Beginner's guide to

TAROT

Beginner's guide to
TAROT

Juliet Sharman-Burke
With cards illustrated by Giovanni Caselli

ST. MARTIN'S GRIFFIN
NEW YORK

To Susie, who gave me my first tarot deck, with love and thanks.

Library of Congress Cataloguing-in-Publication Data available on request.

ISBN-13: 978-0-312-28482-4
ISBN-10: 0-312-28482-9

First St. Martin's Griffin Edition: 2001

3 5 7 9 10 8 6 4

AN EDDISON•SADD EDITION
Edited, designed and produced by
Eddison Sadd Editions Limited
St Chad's House, 148 King's Cross Road
London WC1X 9DH

Phototypeset in Cochin using QuarkXPress on Apple Macintosh
Origination by Pixel Graphics, Singapore
Printed by L Rex, China

CONTENTS

Introduction 6

The Minor Arcana 10

The Suit of Cups 16
Sample Reading for Cups 44

The Suit of Swords 76
Sample Reading for Swords 104

The Suit of Wands 46
Sample Reading for Wands 74

The Suit of Pentacles 106
Sample Reading for Pentacles 134

Sample Reading for Minor Arcana 136

The Major Arcana 141

THE FOOL 142
THE MAGICIAN 144
THE HIGH PRIESTESS 148
THE EMPRESS 148
THE EMPEROR 150
THE HIEROPHANT 152
THE LOVERS 154
THE CHARIOT 156
JUSTICE 158
TEMPERANCE 160
STRENGTH 162

THE HERMIT 164
THE WHEEL OF FORTUNE 166
THE HANGED MAN 168
DEATH 170
THE DEVIL 172
THE TOWER 174
THE STAR 176
THE MOON 178
THE SUN 180
JUDGEMENT 182
THE WORLD 184

Sample Reading for Major Arcana 186

Sample Reading for Complete Deck 189

Acknowledgements 192

Introduction

This book is designed to introduce the beginner to the art of tarot reading. The book accompanies the new Sharman-Caselli deck, which has been inspired in part by the imagery of the famous and very popular Waite deck, created in 1900 by artist Pamela Colman-Smith under the direction of occultist A. E. Waite. The Waite deck marked a significant move away from the earlier decks, the earliest of which dates back to the mid-fifteenth century, by adding pictorial images to the Minor Arcana which had previously been marked by numbers only. The Sharman-Caselli deck has taken some of its imagery from the earliest decks, such as the Visconti-Sfzora, as well as the relatively modern Waite deck. The tarot is an archetypal system, so its images can appeal and be universally understood. The complete tarot comprises seventy-eight cards: twenty-two in the Major Arcana, fifty-six in the Minor Arcana.

The book begins by looking at the Minor Arcana, analysing the individual cards of each suit in turn. There are four suits in the Minor Arcana: Cups, Wands, Swords and Pentacles. These are earlier versions of our modern-day playing-card suits: Hearts, Clubs, Spades and Diamonds. Each suit is connected with one of the four elements, respectively: water, fire, air and earth. In the Sharman-Caselli deck a particular colour and specific symbols are used in the imagery of each suit, linking each one visually with its element. This thematic approach makes it easier for a beginner to identify which suit a particular card belongs to and to connect each suit to its element. To aid further understanding, each of the suits is associated with a particular area of life: the Cups relate to feelings and relationships; the Wands represent creativity and imagination; the Swords relate to life challenges, reflecting the difficulties that we encounter; and the Pentacles represent material and financial aspects of life.

The Court cards of each suit in the tarot comprise a Knight, Queen and King, like a modern playing deck, with the addition of a Page. Each Knight, Queen and King is associated with one of the twelve zodiacal signs and its respective element. This astrological dimension adds depth to their possible interpretations. At the end of the analysis of each suit, a five-card sample spread using only that suit is set out in the Horseshoe layout. This layout will aid the beginner in the interpretation of a combination of cards relating to a specific area of a seeker's life. It is suggested that you practise doing readings with a single suit before moving on. To conclude the Minor Arcana chapter, there is a sample Celtic Cross reading (*see page 156*), using the complete Minor Arcana, including the Court cards, showing you how to combine your understanding of all the suits in a more complex reading.

In the next chapter the cards of the Major Arcana are studied in turn. There are twenty-two cards in the Major Arcana, which together map out the various stages in a person's life. It is useful to think of the procession of the Major Arcana cards as The Fool's journey. The Fool starts the procession. (This card is the only one of the Major Arcana that remains in the modern playing deck as the Joker.) The Fool, like each of us, must pass through childhood and adolescence with all the attendant trials, tribulations, joys and wonderment, and into the adult world where he must eventually face mid-life and the crisis that this so often evokes. The second half of life and the second half of the Major Arcana involves establishing a personal and spiritual world view that is different and more inward-looking than the enthusiasm and activity so often generated in the first half of life. If you attach something of your own experience to each card it will assist your understanding and recognition of it. At the end of this section (*see page 186*) is a sample seven-card Star reading that uses only the Major Arcana. There follows a five-card Horseshoe reading that uses the whole deck (*see page 189*).

Throughout the book I have detailed the symbolism of each card, so that the divinatory meaning of each image can be fully understood. I have also stressed the importance of making a relationship with the image on each card, so that each comes to feel as familiar as an old friend. As you work though each of the cards in turn, I strongly suggest that you try to connect each of the life stages that the cards describe with events that have taken place in your own life. The moment the image becomes personal the card will immediately start to 'speak' to you in an easy and effortless way. It should not be necessary to struggle to try to remember complicated interpretations. If you let the images speak to your unconscious and filter through into your imagination, interpretation will follow naturally.

Always bear in mind that the tarot works through intuition rather than logic. It is therefore essential that you allow your imagination the freedom to wander through the dream world of the tarot pictures in much the same way as a child would approach a fairytale picture book. The tarot images work on an unconscious level; they are like mirrors reflecting knowledge buried in the deepest realms of the mind. That dark, unconscious part of the mind contains knowledge that the conscious mind is unaware of, and the tarot acts as a bridge between the two, using the archetypal nature of the imagery to feed information from unconscious to conscious mind. Answers to all kinds of questions can arise from the unconscious through fantasy, intuitions and dreams, all of which are stimulated by the tarot when it is sensitively and seriously approached.

THE MINOR ARCANA

E ach of the suits in the tarot describes a particular mode of life, which in turn reflects one of the four basic elements of astrology – water, fire, air and earth – and the four psychological types – feeling, intuition, thinking and sensation. To get the most out of the tarot you must be able to understand the symbolism contained within each of the cards, and be able to interpret it. In this section of the book, we look at the symbolism of each suit and the cards within that suit carefully in turn. The Court cards can be tricky to interpret in a reading as they can either represent an actual person entering your life or they can signify an aspect of yourself that needs to be developed. Sometimes they can represent an event.

At the end of the analysis of each suit there is a sample spread that uses only that suit. Practise doing readings using these spreads to become confident in your knowledge of the cards of one suit before moving on to study the next. At the end of the section, there is a sample Celtic Cross spread that uses the whole of the Minor Arcana (*see pages 136–40*), illustrating how to combine all the suits in a single reading.

The Suit of Cups

THEME *Feelings and emotions*

T he suit of Cups describes the shifting and ever-changing world of feelings, and the prime symbol of feelings is the element of water. Like water, feelings are always changing.

You will, I am sure, know from your own experience how you can move from feeling joyful to downcast in a relatively short space of time, often depending on what is going on around you. Water takes the shape of the container it is in. Similarly, both the people around you and the situation you are in can affect the way you feel. Take some time to reflect on the way your feelings ebb and flow. Then imagine water running through different containers. The better you are able to associate the element of water with feelings, the easier you will find it to understand the suit of Cups.

In order to become familiar with the suit of Cups and the element of water, spread the whole suit out in front of you. Allow the symbols, shapes and colours to make an impression on you before you start trying to understand any of the individual cards. Notice that water is always present, whether it takes the form of a river, pool, fountain or ocean. Next, look for other watery symbols depicted in the cards, such as fish or mermaids. Take note of the colours of the suit – watery blues and mauves and pinks – and connect them in your mind with the suit of Cups. The watery suit is cool: try to feel its coolness through the imagery and colours of the cards of this suit. Think how refreshing cold water can be on a hot day, or how relaxing a warm bath is when you are cold or stressed.

Now move on to reading the interpretation of each of the cards in the suit (*see pages 16–43*). A variety of emotions, from joy to sorrow, are covered. It is likely you will recognize the feelings of elation, joy, confusion, doubt and grief, which are all represented in some way by the suit of Cups. The more you are able to connect your own experiences to the images on the cards, the easier it will be to remember their meanings when you want to make an interpretation.

The Suit of Wands

THEME *Imagination and creativity*

The suit of Wands describes the magical process of creativity. One of the prime symbols of creativity is fire. Fire is, if you think about it, pretty magical. A single spark can catch hold of a piece of wood and the next thing you know a bright, blazing, warm fire is roaring. In the same way, the germ of an idea can be kindled by the imagination of one person into a wonderful play or a fabulous picture, or it can be communicated to others, who, in turn, add more wood to the imaginary fire to create something amazing together. Once you have made the connection between fire and the imagination, you are well on your way to understanding the suit of Wands.

Lay out the entire suit of Wands in front of you to gain an impression of the suit in general. Remember that the suit of Wands is primarily about imagination and creativity, and that the prime symbol of creativity is fire. Notice the little flames that appear on each Wand card. The cards contain other symbols of fire and warmth: there is the salamander, the legendary lizard believed to live in flames; sunflowers; and the sun. In addition, every image in the suit of Wands is depicted in the warm, fiery colours of yellow, red, brown and orange, reinforcing each card's connection with fire. Before too long as soon as you see a Wand card you will instinctively associate these symbols with creativity.

Now you are ready to study the individual cards. Each card is shown and described in detail (*see pages 46–73*), allowing you to become familiar with the archetypal imagery and the divinatory meaning. You will soon become aware that the situations depicted in the cards are familiar. The more you are able to connect each situation with a personal experience, the easier you will be able to connect with the cards.

The Suit of Swords

THEME *Life challenges*

The suit of Swords connects to the element of air, which, in turn, connects to the mind, to rational thought and to the creative aspect of mental process. We need the thinking function in order to discriminate, judge and evaluate. To think is to go beyond volatile feelings, instinctive desires and creative visions. The suit of Swords illustrates the various life events that we will all encounter at some time or another, and suggests the application of pure logic and rational analysis to them. The challenges indicated by the Swords are not limited to a single area of life, such as relationships, creativity or finance. The Swords in the tarot more often than not indicate stress or anxiety, which may manifest in any area of life. For example, the Six of Swords is a card that means the moving away from a difficult situation. This may be a problematic relationship, a creative block or a financial muddle. The suit of Swords reflects many of the problems we have in balancing intellect with feelings, intuition and physical needs.

In order to gain a thorough understanding of the suit of Swords, spread all fourteen cards out in front of you and let the images appeal to you visually, first paying attention to the colours. Cool colours, such as ice-blue and steel-grey, reflect the element of air. Remember that the suit of Swords represents difficulties and challenges, as well as solutions through clarity of thought. Now look at the other symbols on the cards, such as birds, butterflies, clouds and the changing patterns of the sky, which all reinforce the idea of the element of air. You will soon become familiar with these images and will associate them with the mind's ability to fly high.

Now move on to reading the interpretation of each of the cards in the suit (*see pages 76–103*). Try to connect your own experiences with each of the cards. The more you are able to do this, the easier it will be to remember their meanings. Once you have attached something personal to each of the cards you will find them unforgettable.

The Suit of Pentacles

THEME *Money and potential*

The suit of Pentacles is linked to the element of earth, which is concerned with the world of form and substance. Every brilliant idea originating with the imaginative Wands must pass through to the Pentacles if it is to be made real. It is all very well having a wonderful idea about a painting or a sculpture, for instance, but it will never amount to anything more than an idea unless it is given concrete form. Giving ideas substance is the domain of the Pentacles. Consider the importance of the material world and in your mind connect it to the element of earth and the suit of Pentacles.

Now spread the entire suit of Pentacles out in front of you to try to get an overall impression of the suit. Remember that the earthy Pentacles are concerned with practical matters and financial issues as you study the individual symbols of earthy reality. Notice that the colours that permeate this suit are those of the earth: brown and green. Notice, too, that the animals portrayed in the Pentacles are mice, rabbits and dogs – all very down-to-earth animals. Other symbols of the earth that appear on the cards of this suit are those of fruit and flowers, bestowed on us by generous Mother Nature and without which we cannot survive.

The symbol of the Pentacles is fascinating in itself. Shaped like a coin, which is a symbol of the material world, it has the magical five-pointed star engraved on it, symbolizing the magical powers of the earth itself. The fact that the earth is able to renew itself each year, and to provide us with nourishment, shelter and beauty, is a magical concept. Yet the magic does not come from the imagination as in the case of the suit of Wands. It comes from the earth itself. To use another analogy, our own physical bodies provide the containers for the ideas represented by the suit of Wands, the feelings highlighted by the suit of Cups and the thoughts symbolized by the suit of Swords.

Now move on to reading the interpretation of each of the cards in the suit (*see pages 106–33*). This will introduce you to the archetypal imagery of each card and its divinatory meaning. As you look closely at each of the images depicted you will begin to recognize familiar situations concerning material and financial issues. As always, the more you are able to connect your own experiences to the images on the cards, the easier it will be to remember their meanings.

ACE *of* CUPS

Element: Water

The clouds
denote a
divine gift

The cup
represents
feelings

The five streams
of water
symbolize the
five senses

The water
lilies stand
for emotional
development

THEME *Upsurge of emotions*

Ahand appears magically from the clouds, bearing a large
golden cup. It comes into the picture from the left, the
side of creativity. The suit of Cups is connected with the
element of water, which symbolizes the feelings. The image on
the Ace is of overflowing water: five separate streams,

representing the five senses, pour out of the cup into the pool of water below. The pool represents the emotions. It is covered with water lilies, a beautiful symbol of emotional growth and development. The magic evoked by powerful feelings is captured in this image.

Divinatory Meaning

All the Aces signify a new beginning. So, in the suit of Cups, the beginning will take place in the emotional life. When this card appears in a reading it can therefore indicate the start of a new relationship, love affair or powerful friendship. Whatever the exact nature of the relationship, there is certain to be a very strong initial attraction.

It is important to remember that the feelings referred to in this card do not necessarily pertain to a sexual relationship; they could also refer, for example, to the intense love that a mother has for her newborn baby. In some situations it can suggest a passionate involvement with a creative idea very close to your heart. Whatever the external situation, the card signifies an upsurge of strong feelings.

Of course, you must take into account that feelings can be both positive and negative. In general, the Ace of Cups is seen as a card that brings joy and contentment in relationships. However, it is important to bear in mind that the emotions evoked when the Ace of Cups is present in a reading could actually be of deep love or deep hate. It is even possible that both could be present at the same time.

TWO *of* CUPS

Element: Water

Winged lion: the wings symbolize spiritual love, the lion sexual love

The white snake stands for wisdom

Red roses represent desire

The black snake stands for healing

White fleurs-de-lys symbolize the spirit

THEME *Friendship*

A woman and a man face one another, exchanging cups. She, standing on the left, represents sensitivity and creativity, while he, standing on the right, represents action. Together they form a balance. They are standing before an arch that is carved with two snakes: the black one on the left represents healing and the white one on the right stands for wisdom. Above the arch is a carved winged lion, symbolizing the balance between spiritual love, signified by the wings, and sexual desire, represented by the lion.

The man wears a blue tunic embroidered with red roses, which represent desire, while the woman wears a long pale blue robe embroidered with the white lilies of the spirit. A narrow stream symbolizing the water element of the suit of Cups can be seen through the arch, winding in the distance.

Divinatory Meaning

The Two of Cups is a card of friendship. The couple are exchanging cups as a symbol of their love and commitment to each other. The exchange of cups indicates their commitment to share with one another, which augurs well for a successful relationship, whether romantic or platonic.

The Two takes the pure emotion of the Ace of Cups and divides it into masculine and feminine, active and passive, to provide duality and a sense of balanced forces. When it appears in a reading, this card suggests the start of a new relationship or the development of a relationship in its early stages. The Two of Cups may also mean reconciliation between warring parties and solutions to disputes. It is most commonly associated with love affairs, but can equally refer to deep and lasting friendships.

Of course, like all the images in the tarot, this card can have a negative connotation: it could suggest the souring of a friendship, or the destruction of a relationship by a negative emotion such as jealousy.

THREE *of* CUPS

Element: Water

Cups are raised in good cheer, indicating joy

Garlands suggest the celebratory aspect of the gathering

The fish is a symbol of water

The pool is an image of the feeling world

THEME *Celebration*

Three girls, wearing long robes in a colour reflecting the water element, dance joyfully. They each hold a cup high in the air in a gesture of celebration and harmony. Their long hair is decorated with flowers as if for a party, and they wear garlands around their waists. They are dancing in a beautiful garden. In the foreground is a fountain with a fish, a symbol of the water element, spouting water into a pool. This suggests the outpouring of emotion.

Divinatory Meaning

Three is the number of initial completion, and in the watery suit of Cups it indicates that something of an emotional nature has been achieved. There is something to be celebrated and an atmosphere of rejoicing.

If the Three of Cups appears in a reading, it could signify an engagement or a wedding, a joyful occasion that marks the culmination of a particular phase: a courtship that has ended in an engagement or an engagement that has reached its climax in a marriage. It could also indicate the birth of a child, or a baptism or naming ceremony. Whatever the event, the message contained in it is clear: enjoy this glad moment but be aware that it represents a peak experience after which the regular struggle of life will necessarily resume. A wedding or birth represents both the moment of culmination and the period of transition from euphoria to the resumption of ordinary life.

This card is not limited to events such as weddings or births. It can apply equally to any joyful time that deserves a celebration, such as important birthdays or anniversaries. The Three of Cups is essentially about the sharing of good times with loved ones.

FOUR *of* CUPS

Element: Water

Clouds mean that he ignores the gifts that are offered to him

Crossed arms and legs indicate blocked and cut-off emotions

The castle represents the positive aspects in his life

The pool of water symbolizes feelings

THEME *Discontent*

A figure wearing a blue tunic and white shirt is sitting on the grass beside a still pool. The water in the pool and the blue of his tunic recall the element of water connected with the suit of Cups. His legs are crossed and his arms firmly folded, indicating his refusal to accept anything that life might be trying to offer him. It appears that he has decided not to open himself up emotionally. He deliberately ignores the golden cup that is being offered to him by a hand that appears magically from a cloud on the right-hand side of the card, the side of action. Instead, he merely stares down in discontent at the three full cups that stand upright in front of him. In the distance, a fine castle can be seen, revealing the extent of the positive factors in his life. Yet still he is unhappy.

Divinatory Meaning

This card is an image of boredom and discontent. After the exceptional joy of the Three of Cups, picking up the reins of routine can seem particularly disagreeable. The feeling inherent in the Four of Cups is primarily one of boredom, and when you feel really bored it is difficult to arouse enthusiasm for anything. The figure in the Four of Cups is clearly unable to appreciate what he does have and is so dissatisfied that he refuses everything, even what is being offered magically. The figure in the card has all he could want and more but he refuses to recognize or acknowledge it.

If this card appears in a reading, it indicates that there is a great deal of value available to you, but if you do not adopt the right attitude nothing much will come of it. The most constructive way of working with this energy is to confront the mood of discontent and examine it closely. Four is the number of reality, and the mixture of reality and feelings may result in apathy. There may be a desire for 'someone else to sort the whole thing out' and, paradoxically, this solution is actually on offer as the magic cup reveals: your senses may have become so dulled that you simply have not noticed.

FIVE *of* CUPS

Element: Water

The black cloak represents sorrow and mourning

The castle stands for hope

The bridge symbolizes the way to move on

The river represents unhappiness

The spilled cups stand for what has been lost

The full cups symbolize what still remains intact

THEME *Regret and sorrow*

A sorrowing figure stands with his back turned, wrapped in a cloak that is black, the colour of grief. Before him three cups are overturned and water is draining out of them. The figure is so intent on the spilled cups that he does not notice the two full cups standing behind him. This suggests that, although something has been lost or spoiled, there is still something remaining that is positive. However, in order to notice this positive element he must turn around.

The mournful figure faces a fast-flowing river, which represents grief and misery. Yet there is a bridge crossing the river, symbolizing the ability to move on. On the other side of the river stands a castle, depicting stability and security and thus hope for the future. The image depicts pain and sorrow, but suggests that all is not lost.

Divinatory Meaning

The Five of Cups represents a period of sorrow. The number Five in the tarot refers to change and difficulty, and in the watery suit of Cups the change is likely to be in the field of the emotions. When this card appears in a reading, it suggests that something has gone wrong on a feeling level, perhaps in a relationship, and there may be regret over past decisions. However, as the image reveals, the emphasis is being placed too heavily on what has been lost rather than on what might be available. The figure gazes only upon the spilled cups without a backward glance at the full cups standing behind him.

It is very common that in moments of disappointment and despair we are only aware of what has been lost and fail to notice what we still have. This card suggests that while something has been lost, there is still something that can be redeemed or used to positive effect. In order to do this it is clear that you need to know how much responsibility you must take for the loss. It is important for you to understand your part in the upset, owning and regretting, if necessary, your actions in the matter.

SIX *of* CUPS

Element: Water

The wishing-
well represents
past wishes

The country
garden
signifies
childhood

The dwarf
symbolizes
the past

The little girl
stands for the
future

The white
lilies denote
innocence
and purity

THEME *Past memories and future dreams*

Six is a number of harmony and in the suit of Cups it suggests gentleness and balance. The image depicts a dwarf
and a little girl arranging flowers in six cups. The little girl
wears a blue dress to recall the watery nature of the Cups, and
symbolizes the future, while the dwarf represents the past;

together they work in the present. They place the flowers, which represent memories, in the cups, which symbolize feelings. In the distance, the thatched cottage and old-fashioned country garden evoke nostalgic feelings of an idyllic childhood, while the wishing well indicates both the water element and past wishes.

Divinatory Meaning

The image shows a young girl and an old dwarf sharing a task, implying that loving relationships can span generations, bringing satisfaction and security. When this card appears in a reading it may indicate that you will receive help from a friend, teacher or family member. It is a benevolent card, conveying a sense of gentleness and calm.

The Six of Cups indicates a time of memory and nostalgia, suggesting that comfort can be drawn from returning to the past when the present is difficult. The Six of Cups also indicates that long-held dreams could become a reality. The wishing well is a symbol of desires, and offers a chance to dream an old dream. This could take the shape of an old love affair rekindling, or a friendship from the past being resurrected in the present. It might also mean that something you have dearly wanted to accomplish for years at last materializes.

The negative aspect of this card is a tendency to live in the past: a totally backward focus can obscure what needs to be done in the present. Past memories can provide comfort and inspiration but if they are used as a dwelling place they may prove to be both inappropriate and unproductive.

SEVEN *of* CUPS

Element: Water

The dragon represents strength

Jewels symbolize wealth

The laurel wreath stands for success

The snake stands for sexuality

The castle symbolizes security

The draped figure represents true self

The dove represents spirit

THEME *Daydreams*

A figure dressed in simple blue robes is lying daydreaming on a bench next to a pool, a symbol of the element of water. Above him are clouds with fantastic visions emerging out of seven gold cups. A dove, which represents the spiritual world, emerges from one cup; a laurel wreath, which denotes success, appears from another; jewels, which symbolize wealth – both material and emotional – arise from a third. The fourth cup produces a fierce dragon, representing strength, while a snake symbolizing sexuality emerges from the fifth. A fine castle arises from the sixth cup, which suggests the promise of security and stability, while the seventh produces a mysterious figure draped in a cloak, an image of the true self waiting to be unveiled and discovered. Together they create an image of vivid imagination, fantasy and fabulous choices.

Divinatory Meaning

The Seven of Cups is a card that offers many options. However, deciding which one to choose can prove quite a challenge. It is a card of fantasy and daydreams, but as they are all 'up in the clouds' nothing will come of these dreams until they are brought into the plane of reality.

Although this is a watery card, the dreams it describes are not restricted to those of romance and relationships. You may have been dreaming of all manner of dreams and wishes when this card appears in a reading, yet the important message it presents is the need to commit yourself to one thing at a time. Unless there is focus and grounding, all the dreams that this card speaks of will remain 'castles in the air' and will never amount to anything tangible.

While the Seven of Cups implies a wide range of potential opportunities, it also contains a drawback, for when anything is possible it becomes difficult to choose, especially when that choice will inevitably involve cutting off possibilities. The downside of the Seven of Cups is that it presents us with too much choice, which can prove as difficult to handle as too little.

EIGHT *of* CUPS

Element: Water

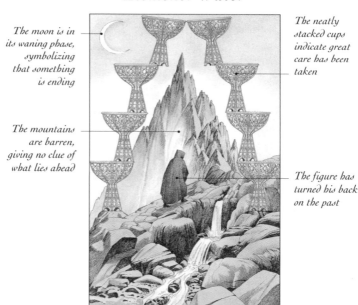

The moon is in its waning phase, symbolizing that something is ending

The neatly stacked cups indicate great care has been taken

The mountains are barren, giving no clue of what lies ahead

The figure has turned his back on the past

THEME *Regeneration*

A figure in a dark blue cloak is climbing up a hill towards a barren peak. He has his back to us. A gentle waterfall runs down the hill beside him, alerting us to the water element and the feeling nature of the suit of Cups. Eight cups are neatly and carefully stacked to form an arch through which the figure has just passed. He is proceeding up towards the barren mountains, indicating a move towards a more meaningful situation. The cups are upright, and appear full, yet they have been abandoned. A waning moon appears in the sky, indicating that something is ending.

Divinatory Meaning

Eight is the number of death and rebirth, or regeneration, so it implies that a change is in the air. When the Eight of Cups appears in a reading, it means that something close to your heart – a relationship, a way of life or perhaps even a project that you loved dearly – is no longer working. It is clear from the image that a great deal of time and energy has been invested in the relationship, for the cups have been arranged lovingly with care and attention. However, care and energy do not, in themselves, mean that the relationship or project will automatically be successful. Just because you try does not necessarily mean you will succeed.

There comes a time, signified by the appearance of the Eight of Cups, when something has run its course and it is time to move on. The figure in the image on this card deliberately turns his back on all he has worked for with the implication that he has had no choice but to abandon the old in favour of the yet unknown new. The upright cups are full yet they are no longer relevant, so the figure walks away, leaving the past behind. Although the image has a sombre air, it heralds a necessary new phase of life. A failure to act at this point could lead to stagnation.

NINE *of* CUPS

Element: Water

The open surroundings symbolize that there is nothing to restrict joy at this moment

The fountains represent an outpouring of emotion

The couple embrace to suggest their love for each other

The feast on the table is an indication of emotional nourishment and sensual satisfaction

THEME *Sensual satisfaction*

The image of the Nine of Cups symbolizes emotional bliss. A young man and woman embrace tenderly as they stand beside a table laden with fruit and flowers, indicating an enjoyment of good things. The table is covered in a pale blue cloth, which is reminiscent of the element of water, and nine full cups are arranged on the table. In the background, the water gardens and sparkling fountains symbolize the constant ebb and flow of feelings. The image suggests a combination of sensual pleasure and emotional satisfaction. It is clearly indicative of a very special moment, a peak experience in life, rather than an everyday occurrence.

Divinatory Meaning

Traditionally, the Nine of Cups is known as the 'wish card', the card that suggests that a dream will be realized or a wish can come true. The nature of the dream is often connected with the emotions and with relationships, but it can also refer to anything that is truly close to your heart.

The Nine of Cups suggests a special time, something out of the ordinary, and a time when sensual pleasures can be indulged, hence the image of a feast laid out in a picturesque setting. The five senses are all catered for in this scene, especially if we imagine the sounds of water splashing from the fountains, music playing, and the smell of good food and fine perfume. Of course, such special peak times do not last indefinitely but they are precious moments, and must be treasured while they last.

When this card comes up in a reading it indicates that the time is ripe to enjoy relationships and to commit yourself fully to realizing a cherished dream. This is not a 'magic' card in that it will not grant the three wishes of a fairytale, but it does indicate that it is a positive time for you to address yourself to making your dreams a reality.

TEN *of* CUPS

Element: Water

The river represents the constant flow of feelings

The house is a symbol of stability

The family group of two males and two females indicates a balance

The garden is an image of fertility

THEME *Contentment and happy home life*

In contrast to the luxurious scene of feasting in the Nine, the Ten of Cups depicts an innocent scene of family unity. A couple embrace as they watch their children play contentedly. The whole group represents harmonious feelings. Ten cups stand upright to form a sort of magic circle around the family and the image is one of ease and enjoyment borne out of contentment in relationships. The garden, symbol of nature's bounty, and house, representing stability, stand securely behind the family. Together the house and garden symbolize a firm foundation, reflecting the effort and care invested in it. A river, which reminds us of the element of water and the feeling nature of the suit of Cups, runs through the landscape, symbolizing the importance of the constant flow of feelings.

Divinatory Meaning

Ten is the number of completion with the One of beginning placed next to the Zero of spirit. So the cycle that is completed in the Ten can return to start a new cycle with the number One. Although the image on the card is one of family unity, its divinatory meaning is not necessarily restricted to family life. In a reading, this card indicates a sense of contentment and emotional fulfilment in relationships of all kinds, whether they are of a romantic, platonic or familial nature.

The feeling tone of this card differs from the bliss found in the Nine in that it represents a more permanent sense of satisfaction and enjoyment of ordinary pleasures. The Ten of Cups indicates contentment rather than ecstasy and it therefore carries a greater sense of permanence than the Nine. The Ten of Cups implies a sense of gratitude for a simple enjoyment in life, such as a loving relationship. It reveals the deep gratification which is found when feelings are shared and appreciated. This card suggests that it requires constant effort to achieve such a state and even more to maintain it. In other words, the benefits illustrated by the Ten of Cups are earned and not magically bestowed.

PAGE *of* CUPS

Element: Water

The fish is an image of the potential for deep understanding of the inner world

The fish patterning on the figure's clothes symbolizes the insights received from deep feelings

The pool represents the emotions

THEME *New beginnings on a feeling level*

All the Pages are represented by youth because they stand for something in its infancy. The Page of Cups depicts a young boy wearing a tunic decorated with fish, a symbol of deep feelings. His clothes reflect the watery colours of the Cups, and he stands by a river, reinforcing the idea of the water element of the suit of Cups. His image is reflected in the water, recalling the way in which we are able to see ourselves reflected in the eyes of others. The Page of Cups holds a gold cup with both hands as though he wishes to grasp all it may offer him. He looks closely at the little fish that is peeping out of the cup at him. The fish is an image of the potential for deep understanding of the inner world. Like a fish, such insights can easily escape, flashing and darting through the deep waters of the emotions, so that only glimpses can be seen at a time.

Divinatory Meaning

When the Page of Cups appears in a reading, it can point to many things. In a literal sense it can bring news of the birth of a child, while on an inner level it can suggest a new beginning in terms of a relationship or the emergence of new feelings within you. It could mean a change of heart about an emotional matter or it could indicate something new in the realm of imagination or artistic talent.

The imagination represented in the suit of Cups is different from that of the Wands in that it is more gentle and sensitive. The creativity of the Cups is less outgoing and exuberant than the fiery Wands; it is more introverted, reflective and passive. The Pages are symbolized by children because the feelings and ideas they indicate are still unformed; the ideas they offer have not reached maturity. They also symbolize a wealth of potential and possibility, which is available in terms of a relationship and on a creative level, although it is still in its very early stages.

KNIGHT *of* CUPS

Element: Water

Winged helmet represents wings of spirit

He holds the cup in his left hand of creativity

Fish are the symbol of Pisces

The river represents the feelings

THEME *The lover*

The Knight of Cups is the personification of a 'knight in shining armour'. He wears a winged helmet and rides a beautiful white horse, walking without haste through the pleasant countryside. The tunic he wears over his shining silver armour is decorated with fish, reflecting the zodiacal sign of Pisces. A wide river, which represents this card's connection with the element of water, meanders through the fields. The Knight of Cups holds his cup before him in his left hand, the side of creativity, and gazes into it intently. He is a romantic idealist, who is ready to do anything in the name of love.

Divinatory Meaning

The Knight of Cups is a quixotic figure, traditionally known as a lover or one who offers marriage. He is essentially a dreamer, who longs for romance and ideal love.

If the Knight of Cups appears in a reading, it may be time for you to pursue your ideals and dreams and your quest for the noble and beautiful in life. The zodiacal sign of Pisces is known for its propensity to sacrifice, especially in the name of love. As Pisces is a water sign, Pisceans have an essentially feeling nature, reacting to situations according to how they feel about something rather than what they think about it. It is certainly a matter of 'heart ruling over head' in the case of both Pisces and the Knight of Cups. Pisceans are often kind-hearted and sympathetic, especially to the underdog, and in their most positive light they are inspirational, resourceful and imaginative. The shadowy side of the sign, and therefore to some extent of the Knight of Cups, is a tendency to be moody, woolly minded and prone to getting lost in a fantasy world.

The appearance of the Knight of Cups in a reading points to the spirit of romance entering your life, which might manifest as a person who matches up to the description of 'lover or seducer' or as an upsurge of romantic or artistic emotions within yourself.

QUEEN *of* CUPS

Element: Water

The crown is made up of fish tails

The oyster-shell throne is a symbol of the depth of feelings

The mermaids symbolize the bridge between the conscious and the unconscious mind

The sea is an image of the vastness of the feeling world

The dolphins symbolize water

THEME *The beloved*

The beautiful Queen of Cups is seated on a throne made out of oyster shells and supported by creatures of the deep, such as dolphins and mermaids. The mermaid is a wonderful image for the Queen of Cups. Half-woman, half-fish, the mermaid bridges the gap between the conscious mortal world and the unconscious – almost magical – sea of the emotions. The Queen of Cups is enthroned in the sea, a clear symbol of emotions, for like feelings, the sea is never the same: sometimes rough and angry, at other times calm and peaceful. Her dress flows like water into the waves at her feet, showing her to be in tune with the depth of her feelings. She gazes thoughtfully into her cup, as she contemplates and processes her emotions.

Divinatory Meaning

The Queen of Cups represents a figure who is profoundly in touch with her emotional world, a world that is of paramount importance to her. This card suggests that any issues relating to feelings are likely to be coming to the fore. This may refer to relationships of any kind, platonic, familial or romantic, and it implies that the feelings are not to be ignored at this time.

The Queen of Cups is connected with the watery sign of Scorpio. Scorpios are known to be passionate and seductive, yet also mysterious and secretive. They are self-contained and intriguing individuals. They are also highly intuitive and tend to trust their instincts completely. Scorpios are also well known for their determination and desire for control. The Queen of Cups wishes for control over her emotions. As an image, the Queen of Cups represents the hypnotic magical power of the feminine world of feelings, alluring and fascinating, yet ultimately unfathomable.

If this card appears in a reading, it could be that someone enters your life whom you find very attractive and magnetic or that you become the beloved of someone else. Alternatively, it may indicate the need to delve into your own feelings to become more aware of what is going on deep within you.

KING *of* CUPS

Element: Water

He holds the
cup in his right
hand of action

The leaping
fish represents
feelings that are
not reined in

The ornamental
fish is a symbol
of feelings kept
in control

The crab crawling
out of the water
connects the King
of Cups to the
sign of Cancer

THEME *One who both loves and fears*

A crowned king sits on a carved throne surrounded by a
troubled sea, but his feet are dry. The ocean represents
the unconscious world of feelings and intuition over which the
conscious mind has no control. While the King of Cups would
like to rule the waves, he knows he cannot do so entirely, so

he is reluctant to allow himself to merge freely with the water. The King of Cups is a powerful figure who sits formally on his stone throne. He holds his cup in his right hand, the side of action, in the same way as he holds the orb, as a symbol of authority. Behind the throne in the distance a fish, representing the power of creativity and imagination, is leaping joyfully out of the water but the King seems unaware of it.

Divinatory Meaning

The King of Cups symbolizes one who wishes to be involved emotionally but is nevertheless cautious about immersing himself in feelings, which are, by their very nature, ambiguous and confusing. In many ways, the watery world of the feelings that the Cups represent is a difficult place for the masculine energy symbolized by the King. Although the Kings in the tarot are not always men (just as the Queens are not always women), the energy they represent is masculine: dynamic, active and straightforward. So when the King of Cups appears in a reading, he suggests that there is a strong desire to be involved intimately with other people, but there is also a fear of the danger in such involvement.

The crab is the symbol of the zodiacal sign of Cancer, and provides a good image for this ambivalence, for crabs belong neither totally on land nor totally in the sea. Such is it with Cancerians, who long for relationships but are fearful of the depth close contact with others may bring. When the King of Cups appears in a reading, it suggests either that someone enters your life who is both compassionate and committed but also quite terrified of deep involvement, or that you may need to confront this aspect of yourself in your own psyche.

Sample Reading for Cups

A young girl called Jemima wanted to know what was in store for her in terms of relationships. She was about to take her final exams at university but still did not know what she wanted to do eventually. She chose the following five cards from the Suit of Cups.

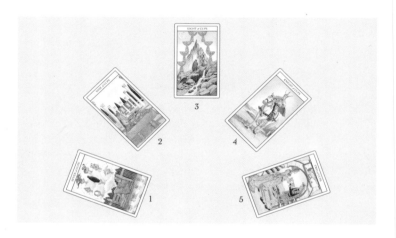

1. Present Position: Seven of Cups

The Seven of Cups suggests many dreams and possibilities, which will always remain dreams unless action is taken. Jemima did indeed have a number of ideas about what she wanted to do but she felt she could not put anything into practice until she had the results of her degree.

2. Present Expectations: Nine of Cups

This card signifies that a wish of paramount importance can come true. Jemima was torn between a wish for good exam results and a longing for the man she was currently in love with to marry her.

3. What is Unexpected: Eight of Cups

The Eight of Cups is a card that denotes leaving behind something you have put a great deal of time and energy into because it is not working. When we discussed this card, Jemima thought that it might refer to her current relationship. This was her first serious love affair and she had put her heart and soul into it, yet her efforts did not seem to be truly appreciated or even fully reciprocated. It was very hard for her to contemplate turning her back on it, yet she was also able to see that it was not working in the way she would ideally like.

4. Immediate Future: Knight of Cups

This card indicates the chance of romance and a new relationship entering Jemima's life. It also suggests that perhaps she should try to develop her own ideas on romance and relationships and explore those more before deciding to settle down. She agreed that she may be too young to rush into marriage, although the idea did appeal to her greatly.

5. Long-term Future: Two of Cups

This is a card that suggests a relationship based on friendship and equality. The Two of Cups indicates a healthy balance between opposites and denotes a relationship based on sharing and giving.

Conclusion

Jemima's dreams need to be narrowed down, so that she can choose just one to make real (Seven of Cups). Although something that she wishes for may come about (Nine of Cups), she also needs to be more objective about her current relationship and assess it realistically (Eight of Cups). She may begin a new relationship (Knight of Cups), which might encourage her to analyse her own feelings more deeply and honestly. This, in turn, may help her to establish a good relationship (Two of Cups) in the longer term.

ACE *of* WANDS

Element: Fire

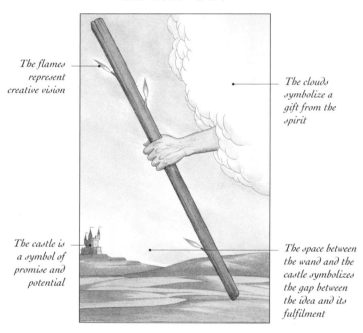

The flames represent creative vision

The clouds symbolize a gift from the spirit

The castle is a symbol of promise and potential

The space between the wand and the castle symbolizes the gap between the idea and its fulfilment

THEME *Outburst of creativity*

A hand emerges from the clouds, offering a single wand. This is the image of a gift from above. The wand has three small flames, symbolizing the fire of creativity, imagination and vision. These three sparks are essential if anything inspired is to emerge into the material world. The Wand is tilted slightly to the left, the side of creativity. The landscape is open and empty; the sky is clear and untroubled. In the distance is a castle, a symbol of future promise. Between the wand and the castle is space, which symbolizes the gap between the idea and the fulfilment of the idea in reality.

Divinatory Meaning

The suit of Wands suggests action, movement and creativity, and the Aces, or number Ones, symbolize a new start. So the Ace of Wands signifies a beginning full of energy and initiative. The Wands are linked to the element of fire, which is restless, adventurous and full of ideas. So the Ace of Wands indicates that the time is ripe for a new creative endeavour, which might be artistic, but might equally be a new endeavour in the business world. Whatever line it takes, the essential ingredient required to get a new project underway is the primary spark of inspiration symbolized by the Ace.

The positive aspect of the Ace of Wands is the enormous enthusiasm and optimism it represents in abundance. But it is crucial to remember that any new idea needs careful nurturing if it is to come to fruition. In other words, simply having the idea is not enough; there must be a connection between the Wand and the castle.

When this card appears in a reading, it is likely that you will encounter an upsurge of energy and initiative in respect of a new undertaking of some kind. This new project could take the form of anything from an artistic endeavour to the founding of a company.

TWO *of* WANDS

Element: Fire

The right-hand wand indicates action and the left-hand wand symbolizes passivity, while the figure acts as the balance between the two

The steps down to the water represent the path that is mapped out

Salamanders represent the element of fire

Cloak and boots signify a journey

THEME *Work is under way*

Aman stands looking out over harbour walls towards the sea beyond. The ocean is a symbol of the uncharted waters that lie ahead at the beginning of any new venture. Gazing out over the ocean often evokes a sense of wonder tinged with fear about what will emerge from its depths. The figure holds a wand in each hand: one is tilted slightly to the right, signifying action, and the other is tilted to the left, signifying creativity. Together they indicate balanced forces. The man is about to start a journey, the idea for which originated in the Ace. Enough groundwork and planning has been carried out to make the idea viable. Carved in the wall are two salamanders, those legendary lizards believed to live in fire, to remind us of the fiery nature of the suit.

Divinatory Meaning

The Two of Wands is a card of duality. The single idea that emerged in the Ace has now split into two. The Two of Wands symbolizes the balance between action and passivity, which is indicated by the two wands held one in each hand, right and left. The combination of the two wands indicates equilibrium.

However, the essential message of this card is of potential that is yet to be fulfilled. When this card comes up in a reading, it suggests that some decisions have been taken and preparations made, but the journey has not actually been started. The figure stands on the walls dressed for travel in boots and cloak, holding two wands, indicating what has already been achieved. The view over the horizon hints at what is yet to come. It is a card of energy and enterprise, suggesting enthusiasm and passion, yet balance.

At best, the Two of Wands indicates a new venture that is launched from a firm foundation. At worst, it might indicate a tendency always to be planning but never actually taking the first step. When this card appears in a reading it is likely that you will be faced with many opportunities for the future but the outcome is still far from clear.

THREE *of* WANDS

Element: Fire

The firmly placed wands indicate that a project is well on its way

The pyramids stand for ancient wisdom

The ships represent the imagination

The salamander symbolizes the magic of the element of fire

THEME *Completion of the first phase*

A man gazes out over the water as the ships of his ideas sail confidently towards their destination. The pyramids in the distance symbolize ancient knowledge and wisdom. Three wands are placed firmly in the ground, signifying achievement, and the man stands firm in the knowledge that his vision will be realized. The tiny flames on the wands represent a creative vision that never fades. The figure continues to wear the cloak and boots of travel because, although he has achieved much, his journey is still in its early stages. The surrounding landscape is sandy, recalling the fiery heat of the sun, and barren, suggesting that nothing is totally fixed and opportunities for new projects have not all been realized.

Divinatory Meaning

Three is the number of initial completion. The Three of Wands suggests that the first stage of an enterprise has been reached. The idea born in the Ace is set to work in the Two, resulting in an achievement in the Three. When this card comes up in a reading, it often applies to someone who has set out to achieve something and has fixed on a particular goal, thinking of it as the end result. Sometimes, however, it transpires that the point originally considered to be the end turns out in reality to be only the beginning. The Three of Wands describes this kind of experience. Having reached the initial completion it becomes clear that there is still a long way to go, and much more to do and discover, before a real end to the journey will be in sight.

This revelation can be either disappointing or exciting, depending on how you feel about the prospect. The element of fire responds positively to inspiration, and, in fact, the vision and the challenge can sometimes be more exciting than the final achievement. The result achieved in the Three of Wands is satisfying but by no means is it the end of the road.

FOUR *of* WANDS

Element: Fire

Oranges are a solar and thus fiery fruit

The wreath is a symbol of success

The decorative garlands denote a celebration

The four wands symbolize security and stability

THEME *A time to reap rewards*

Four is a number of stability. This card shows a canopy of fruit and flowers supported by four wands, which are firmly rooted in the ground, symbolizing a secure base. A figure stands beneath the canopy, raising a wreath above his head in a gesture of triumph. The same journeying figure appeared in the Two and Three of Wands. In the Four he is pictured taking a welcome break to indulge in some well-earned praise before moving on to the next stage. The garlands symbolize a time of celebration and reward. In the distance stands a castle, representing accomplishment and achievement, which is well within reach. Crowds come forth to greet him and welcome him home. The salamander reminds us of the fiery nature of this card.

Divinatory Meaning

The Four of Wands offers a prize. There is a sense of well-deserved reward and exhilaration that emanates from this joyful image. In a reading, the message of the fruit-laden garlands depicted may indicate a time of celebration and congratulation, following a period of hard labour or effort. Traditionally, it is known as the 'harvest home', the feast following the weeks of work involved in bringing in the crops.

As the suit of Wands is a fiery one, the Four of Wands often describes the joyful moment when a creative venture, having passed through the first stages of inspiration and initial painstaking work, suddenly becomes a viable entity. It could be likened to the moment an investment starts to pay out dividends for you. However, the Four appears early in the suit, so, although it indicates initial success, it also intimates that there are yet more mountains to climb. The Four of Wands allows only a brief holiday period of rest and relaxation before continuing with life's journey. The warning note contained in this card is to be wary of basking in the warm glow of success for too long.

FIVE *of* WANDS

Element: Fire

The flames on the wands symbolize the creative element of fire

The crossed wands show the difficulties and blocks that stand in the way of the imagination

The salamander represents the creative nature of the aspirations

THEME *Struggle and frustration*

In general, the number Five in the tarot is indicative of strife and irritation. The image of five men struggling in evident conflict captures this notion quite clearly. However, it is important to note that the men do not appear to be trying to harm each other seriously. There is much brandishing of wands, and even close combat, but no blood is shed, nor will there be. This image is aggressive and obviously symbolizes annoyance and irritation, but it is not mortally dangerous. The clashing wands suggest a time of creative frustration, while the fact that one of the men is wearing no shoes suggests vulnerability. The familiar emblem of fire – the salamander – reminds us that the subject of the struggle is in the area of artistic vision, inspiration and creative aspiration.

Divinatory Meaning

When the Five of Wands appears in a reading, it is likely that you will be experiencing a time of frustration and annoyance, particularly in relation to creative or artistic projects.

The Five of Wands suggests a period of time when everything seems to be conspiring against you and no matter how hard you try, harsh reality seems to continually stand in the way of creative vision. This card can describe the occurrence of the classic writer's or artist's block. It is a time of petty irritations, which do not really matter in the greater scheme of things but can be rather exhausting all the same. Perhaps the best way of describing the quality of this phase is the phrase 'taking one step forward and two steps back'.

Making progress is neither smooth nor easy when this card comes up, with communication both at work and in personal relationships proving tricky and confusing. However, on a more positive note, this phase will not last forever, and it is often the case that frictions and frustrations force us into new, and sometimes more constructive, ways of doing things.

SIX *of* WANDS

Element: Fire

The laurel leaf crown is a symbol of success and victory

The salamander decoration reminds us that the achievement could be linked to creativity

The crowds cheer; a public acknowledgement of achievement

THEME *Public acclaim and success*

The Six in the tarot is a number of harmony and balance, which often suggests that a cycle has reached the point of completion. A figure on horseback is crowned with the laurel wreath of success, holding aloft a wand adorned with another wreath of fruit and foliage. Behind him follow his band of loyal supporters, all holding high their wands in joy and triumph. The scene is one of victory and the image suggests that adversity has, for the time being anyway, been overcome. The flames on the wands, and the salamanders decorating the horse's harness, call to mind the fiery element of this suit, so the achievement indicated is likely to be in the area of creativity.

Divinatory Meaning

The Six of Wands is a card that suggests that a moment of public acclaim or glory has been achieved. The emphasis is on recognition and endorsement by others, rather than a personal sense of satisfaction. It is as though the world has judged something and found it worthwhile, so it becomes part of the public domain. An obvious example of such a situation would be the publication of a book, or the release of a film or CD, but just as relevant could be a promotion at work. In this case, your work, which is of a high standard, has come to the attention of those in authority who then raise your profile in the company. This card describes a public achievement, not some good works that have been carried out behind closed doors.

The potential for difficulty in this card lies in the fact that public acclaim can easily turn into public criticism. You can become infamous just as quickly as you become famous.

SEVEN *of* WANDS

Element: Fire

The wands symbolize creative ideas

The figure beating off the wands suggests conflict or struggle, but of an internal nature

The figure is battling with his own creativity, so he needs no protection such as boots or cloak

THEME *Stiff competition*

Seven is the number of depth and wisdom. The image shows a solitary figure holding up a single wand against six other wands, which appear to be attacking him from nowhere: there are no other figures present. The figure is surrounded but untouched. The image is powerful and active but does not suggest violence or real fear. The figure is battling with his own creative forces, which he needs to improve and to master. He wears no boots, only shoes, and no cloak: these protective items do not help when you are battling with your own ideas. He must face himself without such safeguards, and it is not easy.

The usual symbols of the flames and the salamander appear in the card to remind us that we are dealing with the fiery world of the imagination. The colour red, which is prominent, reminds us of the issue of creativity raised in this image.

Divinatory Meaning

The traditional meanings of this card include competition and the courage needed to face that competition. Success and public acclaim were achieved with the Six of Wands; the Seven of Wands indicates the next step, which is the need to keep the momentum going.

Once something is accomplished you cannot simply sit back and relax. After a success or a promotion, much more is expected of you. The more you achieve, and the better you do, the more you have to live up to, and this card suggests that the time is ripe for struggle to improve on past achievements.

If this card appears in a reading it can indicate a change in profession, which may call for increased strength and determination. The figure on the card is struggling alone; he is fighting himself as much as any external forces. He is not being judged by the outside world as harshly as he is struggling with his own image of himself. This card suggests healthy and creative conflict, which can be extremely productive. The difficulties this card suggests include becoming bogged down in detail and losing sight of the goal.

EIGHT *of* WANDS

Element: Fire

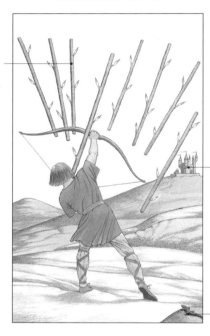

The wands flying through the air suggest new directions

The castle in the distance signifies hopes and wishes

The salamander represents optimism and creative vision

THEME *Action and excitement*

The image is of a figure shooting his bow from which eight wands fly freely through the sky. The archer's posture and position indicate activity and verve while the flaming wands symbolize the creative element of fire. Their flight into so many different directions indicates the vast possibilities that are available. The wands denote inspiration and plenty of ideas, and the broad landscape reveals there is sufficient space in which they can all expand. The castle on the hill suggests the goal to be aimed for, even though it is in the distance. The scene is active and positive, full of optimism and enthusiasm. The familiar image of the salamander symbolizes fire.

Divinatory Meaning

The Eight of Wands is a card that suggests energy and a keen desire for expansion. The fiery wands are quite literally 'in their element' when combined with the Eight, the number of regeneration. The wand arrows flying from the bow of the figure indicate new beginnings in areas such as business or creative ventures, heralding hopes and dreams. The time for waiting is over and it is now 'full speed ahead'.

There are phases in life when it is appropriate to wait and watch but this is not one of them. When the Eight of Wands is prominent in a reading, it indicates a busy, productive period, full of excitement, travel, communication and adventure. As the image shows, the arrows of ideas fly fast and furious towards the castle of fulfilment, filling the sky with masses of possibility and potential.

When this card comes up in a reading, it suggests activity and action, the end of delays and a time when fortune is on your side. The negative message inherent in this card is that nothing may actually come to fruition. It can describe the kind of situation in which there is endless activity but nothing ever seems to reach a satisfactory conclusion.

NINE *of* WANDS

Element: Fire

The eight wands show what has been achieved

The bandage symbolizes an injury to ideas or creative vision

The ninth wand defends the achievement

THEME *Inner strength*

Nine is the number of strength, and the image on this card shows a fighting figure who appears to be defending his territory. Although the enemy cannot be seen, it seems clear that the figure feels he is under attack and is prepared to defend what is dear to him. It is evident that his visions have received a blow because his head, symbolizing the seat of ideas, is wounded, yet he refuses to surrender. The figure stands firm, apparently courageous and determined in the face of adversity. The presence of the fiery salamander reminds us that the issues at stake are most likely to be creative ones, as does the red colour of his tunic.

Divinatory Meaning

The appearance of the Nine of Wands in a reading suggests inner strength and determination. The situation that you find yourself in may be perilous and the demands high, yet you do have enough internal resources to battle through, even though you may doubt yourself. The innate competitiveness of the fiery wands indicates that no matter how difficult or dangerous a situation may be, it is always worth trying to 'fight the good fight'.

This card indicates that you have an accumulation of strength and courage, which can be drawn upon in critical times. It speaks of internal resources rather than a reliance on the outside world to rescue you in times of trouble. This card suggests that you will be called upon to use your integrity and innate courage to free yourself from hardships and opposition. Perhaps the most important aspect of this card is its reliance on wisdom gained through personal experience, which is, after all, the most valuable kind. This card always indicates a struggle but it also always carries the hope of victory, no matter how impossible this may appear at first glance.

TEN *of* WANDS

Element: Fire

The wands are bundled together to form a heavier burden than necessary

The road to the city is winding and not straightforward

THEME *Oppressive burdens*

The figure depicted on this card is struggling with an obviously heavy and rather awkwardly held bundle of wands. The city he is aiming to reach seems very far away, and there is little joy in the image. The fiery creativity inherent in the suit of wands, symbolized as always by the salamander, has become burdensome. The wands are no longer free; there is no space between any of them. Instead they are all lumped together to form a huge and hefty load.

The normally spirited wands are subdued in the Ten. Yet if you look at the image closely, there is no reason why the bundle should be carried in this way. The man is quite free to organize his burden however he likes but he chooses to carry them in such a way that he cannot see where he is going.

Divinatory Meaning

The Ten of Wands is a card that epitomizes the negative aspect of the fire element, which lies in a desire not to believe that boundaries or limitations exist. The fiery wands generally like to think they can do anything they fancy without adverse consequences. However, the Ten of Wands depicts graphically what can happen if the limits are overreached. His bundle traps the figure in the image yet there is nothing to suggest that he has been forced to carry his load in this way.

An example of how this card could manifest itself might be in the artist who enthusiastically takes on many commissions and then finds himself physically unable to carry out the work. The ideas and the desire to create are greater than the physical capacity to do so. This card suggests that creative joy and excitement has become trapped in mundane reality, so it is no longer exciting and enjoyable but instead feels oppressive and arduous. Of course, there is a solution to the dilemma but it is not the magical kind that most appeals to the fiery wands. On the contrary, the solution lies in taking time to lay down the burdens and then slowly work out a more comfortable and effective way of carrying them to the city.

PAGE *of* WANDS

Element: Fire

Wand tilts to
the left of the
card, suggesting
creativity

Right hand
symbolizes
action

The salamander,
symbol of fire,
is close to the
figure's heart

The suns on the
figure's tunic
represent fire

THEME *A messenger bringing creative ideas*

The Pages are represented by young people because they symbolize the suit in its simplest form. The Page of Wands stands proud and optimistic in a sun-drenched landscape, which is reminiscent of the fiery element of this suit. In his right hand, the side of action, he is holding a wand that tilts to the left of the card, the side of creativity, thus combining action and creativity. His cloak is brightly decorated with embroidered suns, themselves symbols of fire, and is trimmed with salamanders, the legendary lizards that live in flames. His breastplate is adorned with a large salamander. In his cap is a long feather, symbolizing truth. The young man stands firm, looking out over the horizon. All the Pages in the tarot are messengers, spreading news and imparting information.

Divinatory Meaning

The Page of Wands is depicted as a child because he symbolizes something in its infancy. Children are known to be frank and uninhibited with an eagerness to learn that is positively infectious. In a similar way, the Page of Wands inspires all those around him. There is great potential in all the Pages but, as with anything young and fragile, this potential needs to be nurtured and protected. The suit of Wands describes the imagination and creative mind, so the Page of Wands suggests that something new and embryonic in this field is emerging.

When the Page of Wands appears in a reading, a person may enter your life and inspire you to become involved with creative ventures. Alternatively, the inspiration may come through study or learning, particularly subjects that stimulate the imagination and encourage artistry. Although the impact of the Ace is much more powerful, the Page also represents the initial spark of interest, the flame of which, once fanned, can grow into something important. The saying 'from tiny acorns mighty oak trees grow' is apt when applied to the Page. For example, a seemingly insignificant idea may turn into a bestselling novel, or blockbuster movie.

KNIGHT *of* WANDS

Element: Fire

The feather represents a search for truth

Salamanders as a symbol of fire decorate the horse's harness

The suns symbolize the warmth of fire

The pyramids symbolize knowledge

THEME *Energy and action*

The image of the Knight of Wands is one of speed, movement and animation. The horse's hooves do not even touch the ground as the Knight gallops across the sun-baked plains.

The symbols of the fiery element of the suit of Wands are plentiful: the lining of the Knight's cloak is decorated with blazing suns, while embroidered salamanders trim his horse's harness. A large red feather flies triumphantly from his helmet. The overall impression created by this image is one of energy and enthusiasm. The pyramids in the distance symbolize ancient wisdom, which the Knight leaves behind in search of new knowledge. He holds high his flaming wand, a symbol of the imagination, which is what he values most. Like all the Knights, he is on a quest.

Divinatory Meaning

The Knight of Wands is a wonderfully extravagant figure. He is an adventurer by nature and possesses such qualities as strong intuition, a vivid imagination and the ability to make the ordinary into something extraordinary.

When the Knight of Wands appears in a reading, he usually brings about changes, in external or internal ways, and sometimes both. If the Knight of Wands represents a person entering your life, he is a volatile, exuberant character, immensely creative and confident. In fact, he is so confident that it never occurs to him that he may fail, so he takes risks and chances without batting an eyelid. As a result of this supremely positive attitude he is often highly successful, and if he is not, he is quick to pick himself up and start something else. He is not given to brooding or regret. The Knight of Wands can be connected with the zodiacal sign of Sagittarius, the seeker of knowledge. If this card represents an aspect of yourself, it may be that you need to develop some of the fiery optimism and enthusiasm embodied in it and meet life with a smile rather than a frown. If this card signifies an event, it is often one connected with moving – home, job or even country.

QUEEN *of* WANDS

Element: Fire

The throne suggests her position in the world

The sunflower is a symbol of her femininity

The wand in her right hand suggests her powerful position

The fiery zodiacal sign Leo is connected with lions

The cat signifies her commitment to home life

THEME *Generosity and strength*

The Queen of Wands is regal figure seated in a throne richly carved with all the symbols of the fiery suit of Wands. Two carved lions, representing the zodiacal sign Leo, form the arm rests of her throne and flames and salamanders decorate its back. At her feet sits a real cat, a symbol of domesticity, for this Queen can combine home life with position in society. She holds a sunflower, symbol of fire, in one hand, and a wand, signifying her majesty and position of power, in the other.

Divinatory Meaning

The Queen of Wands is a interesting mix of fiery enthusiasm, optimism and ambition. She has a sincere wish for relationships and a satisfying home life. Unlike the Knight of Wands, the Queen is not prepared to take risks. She is happy to gamble when she is sure that she can win. She minds losing much more than the Knight of Wands, so she learns her limitations and operates within them.

The Queen of Wands is connected with the zodiacal sign of Leo, which is both fiery and fixed, so there is a sense of boundary connected with the Queen of Wands that is not as evident in the Sagittarian Knight or the Aries King. When it appears in a reading, the Queen of Wands may represent someone entering your life who is capable of attending to many different areas of life at the same time. She is simultaneously available to the family, successful and powerful at work and interested in creative or artistic pursuits. If this card suggests an aspect of yourself that you need to develop, it might include versatility and creativity. The Queen of Wands is a generous friend and willing to share any good fortune. She possesses such qualities as loyalty and dependability yet at the same time she does not suffer fools gladly and can become impatient if she feels she is being used. She enjoys admiration and is happy to be centre stage. If she represents an event, it is likely to be a lucky break, an opportunity that must be seized with both hands.

KING *of* WANDS

Element: Fire

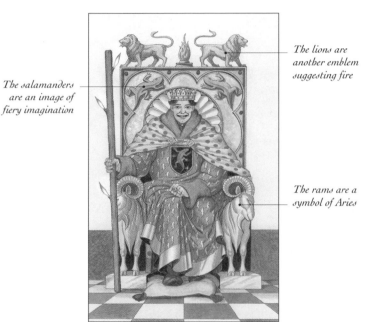

The lions are
another emblem
suggesting fire

The salamanders
are an image of
fiery imagination

The rams are a
symbol of Aries

THEME *Charismatic leader*

The King of Wands is seated on a throne carved with fiery symbols, such as lions and salamanders, with two rams forming the arm rests. The ram is the astrological symbol of the zodiacal sign of Aries, which is associated with the King of Wands. He sits with one foot forward as though he is eager to be up and doing things, and he uses his wand as a staff to help him on his way rather than as a symbol of power and majesty. His robe is decorated with salamanders, symbolizing the fiery attributes of drama and imagination.

Divinatory Meaning

The King of Wands is an active, restless, impatient spirit, anxious to experience every possible aspect of life. He is a born leader, not so much because he craves power but because he has visions that he shares enthusiastically with those around him, who are then inspired to follow him. He is great fun to be around, if somewhat exhausting, and his positive outlook encourages others to gravitate towards him. However, he is also inconsistent, rather irritable if events do not go his way and intolerant of losing.

The King of Wands is ambitious and competitive. His main talent lies in his ability to encourage others, and he makes an excellent salesman or politician. He believes absolutely in himself and assumes that others will automatically follow him. His supreme confidence inspires trust in others, so he usually has a band of admirers. They may not stay long in his court, however, because the King of Wands, like many Arians, gets bored easily and does not like having the responsibility of other people's demands or expectations on his shoulders.

In a reading, the King of Wands might mean that such a person may enter your life, or that you need to develop the 'can-do' qualities embodied in this card along with a confident and positive outlook that may encourage you to take risks or make changes. As an event, this card may suggest that artistic or creative projects come to fulfilment.

Sample Reading for Wands

A forty-five-year-old businessman called George came to see me regarding the likelihood of success in his working life. He chose the following five cards from the Suit of Wands.

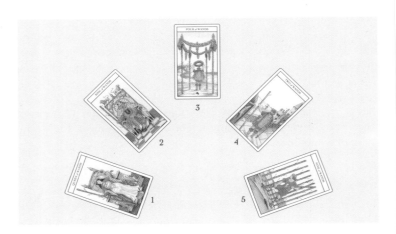

1. Present Position: Queen of Wands

This card describes a person who manages to keep several different projects going at once as well as paying attention to personal and family life. George told me that he is self-employed and manages several different businesses. He also has a wife and three children, and he is keen not to ignore his family.

2. Present Expectations: King of Wands

This is a fiery card and suggests someone who loves to inspire others with new ideas. The King of Wands can indicate a salesman. This was most appropriate in George's case as he was currently in the process of trying to introduce a new idea into a large company. Negotiations were under way, but the deal was not finalized. Nevertheless, the enthusiasm and energy represented by the King of Wands bodes well.

3. *What is Unexpected: Four of Wands*

The Four of Wands suggests reward after hard labour. In this position, the card seemed to indicate that the outcome of George's deal would be positive. However, the Four of Wands also means that once the good cheer is over, George will have to continue with the hard work.

4. *Immediate Future: Two of Wands*

This card indicates that a journey is about to be taken. George felt that this meant that winning the contract would mean the beginning of a long journey.

5. *Long-term Future: Nine of Wands*

The Nine of Wands suggests that a difficult time lies ahead, yet also indicates that there will be strength in reserve. George agreed that getting the deal accepted would be the easy part and that to keep the whole project running would take a great deal of energy and time.

Conclusion

It seemed that to make progress in his work George would need to be very flexible and versatile (Queen of Wands) and let his enthusiasm and optimism bring his ideas to life (King of Wands). He would then be in a position to enjoy a momentary period of celebrating success (Four of Wands). After that he would need to start a new journey into the unknown (Two of Wands), armed with a certain amount of knowledge, which would then be put to the test (Nine of Wands). Although this journey would be exacting, George would have enough inner strength and reserve of energy to win through.

ACE *of* SWORDS

Element: Air

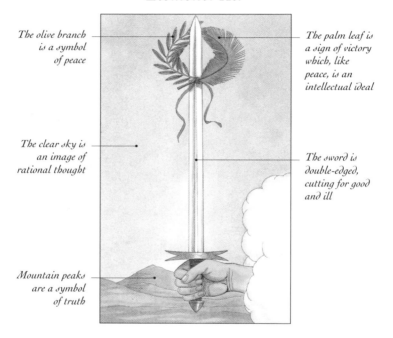

The olive branch is a symbol of peace

The palm leaf is a sign of victory which, like peace, is an intellectual ideal

The clear sky is an image of rational thought

The sword is double-edged, cutting for good and ill

Mountain peaks are a symbol of truth

THEME *The old order changes*

The Ace of Swords shows an upright sword, which suggests truth, encircled by a wreath made up of the olive branch of peace and the palm leaf of victory. The hand holding the sword emerges from the right-hand side of the card, the side of action. The wreath itself is a symbol of attainment and achievement. The sword is double-edged, which means it can cut two ways, for good or ill, so its appearance is always powerful. The element of air connected with the suit of Swords is shown in the clear blue sky, while the plain mountain peaks represent a quest for truth, and indicate that the mind is always seeking perfection and rational understanding.

Divinatory Meaning

The Ace of Swords is a powerful card that heralds a dramatic new beginning, something it shares with the other Aces. The Ace of Swords, the suit connected with challenges, indicates the possibility of some interesting new circumstances. One of the traditional meanings of this card is 'out of something evil something good will come'.

When the Ace of Swords appears in a reading, it can bring with it a sense of sweeping change, which may seem disruptive yet is often necessary. However, it is important to remember that out of the chaos something positive can emerge. A situation that may seem initially negative or unhelpful may turn out to be a blessing in disguise. All the Swords are connected with the intellect, which searches for truth and justice. The element that is linked with the Swords is air, which symbolizes the ability to think and conceptualize that is peculiar to human beings. This ability makes life more interesting but not necessarily easier.

TWO *of* SWORDS

Element: Air

The new moon
shows that
tension is
mounting

The blindfold
signifies
deliberate
obscuring of
truth

The mountains
and rocks
indicate hard
facts of reality

The crossed
swords indicate
protection from
painful feelings

The sea
represents
turbulent
emotions

THEME *Tension and anxiety*

The Two of Swords depicts a blindfolded figure seated with her back to a rough sea. She is holding two large swords crossed over her heart, suggesting that she has deliberately attempted to cut off her feelings. She is wearing a blindfold that she has tied herself with the intention of blocking her vision. Her back is turned on the turbulent sea of emotions yet the mountains and cold rocks of hard fact jut out nonetheless. The swords are perfectly balanced yet look very heavy; the image is one of tension and fear. The moon is in its first quarter, symbolizing growing tension, while a stiff breeze is blowing in the background, emphasizing the element of air.

Divinatory Meaning

Two is the number of opposites, which must be held in balance. In the suit of Swords, which represents the challenges life presents us with, this card speaks of a desire to be shielded from difficult decisions. It may be that the seeker is in a situation that is full of conflict, yet wishes to ignore the strife, perhaps hoping that if it is not acknowledged, the difficulties will somehow go away. It is clear from the image that much effort is being put into keeping the troublesome facts of the matter from view: the figure has turned her back on the situation, crossed her heart in an attempt to protect herself from painful feelings, and she has placed a blindfold over her eyes, so that the truth may be obscured. However, there is so much tension in this image it is also clear that trying to hide from reality cannot go on indefinitely either.

If this card appears in a reading, try to understand what the conflict is about. If the situation can be opened out and the fear honestly faced, something can be done to resolve the issue. What is unacknowledged cannot be changed.

THREE *of* SWORDS

Element: Air

Doves symbolize peace and healing

Halo of light offers hope

The heart pierced with swords is symbolic of the heart pierced with sorrow

THEME *Tension released*

The Three of Swords shows a heart pierced with three swords in a stained glass window. Storm clouds in different shades of blue and purple fill the rest of the stained glass image, suggesting the threat of pain or sorrow. The motifs of birds and butterflies at the bottom and in and around the edge of the stained glass window connect the Three of Swords with the element of air. The halo of light surrounding the heart at the centre of the window gives hope, shining like a candle in the dark. In the top corners of the window, doves symbolize peace and healing.

Divinatory Meaning

The Three of Swords is quite obviously a vision of sorrow and pain. The image of a heart pierced by three swords does not leave a great deal to the imagination when interpreting this card. We all know that heartache is an inevitable and unavoidable part of life, and while it is agony at the time we know, too, that the heart heals with time. There is a sense of peace and calm about the beautiful stained glass window containing the sorrowful image of a wounded heart. Tarot author and expert Rachel Pollack has suggested that to true sorrow we can make only one response – take the pain into our hearts, accept it and go beyond it. There are times and circumstances when something must end or change. The Three of Swords symbolizes the pain such an occurrence involves.

When this card appears in a reading, it heralds some form of strife, disappointment or sadness, yet there is also an underlying sense of understanding that it is inevitable, perhaps even necessary in some way. After the tension of the Two of Swords, there is a resolution in the Three. Although it may seem a glib comment to make when someone is suffering, joy and sorrow do come from the same place and they are never far apart, although they rarely sit down together.

FOUR *of* SWORDS

Element: Air

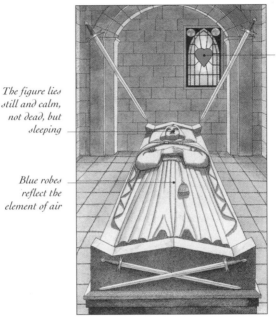

The figure lies
still and calm,
not dead, but
sleeping

Blue robes
reflect the
element of air

The image of
sorrow from the
Three of Swords
has moved to
the background,
representing the
healing process
in motion

THEME *Recuperation and convalescence*

The image of the Four of Swords is of a crypt containing a stone tomb carved with two swords. A further two swords point down to the figure lying on top of the tomb. A figure in blue robes is lying sleeping on his back, eyes closed with hands clasped on his chest. Above, in the right-hand corner, is a stained glass window depicting the red heart of the Three of Swords but without the swords. The colours are grey and stone. The image is not of death but of rest.

Divinatory Meaning

Four is the number of stability, and in the suit of Swords, which so often refers to challenge or strife, it translates as a time for recuperation and recovery. After the heartache of the Three of Swords, the Four of Swords depicts a time of rest and healing. When this card appears in a reading, it heralds a time of relaxation or release of tension, which might follow a time of emotional strain or unhappiness. Alternatively, it might suggest the need for a time for convalescence after an illness. In today's busy and stress-filled world we tend to undervalue the importance of relaxation after periods of intense activity or recovery after illness.

The image on the Four of Swords is one of total calm and quiet, showing a figure in complete repose. Although the image may appear cold, it does not symbolize death but rather tranquillity and peaceful sleep. Your mind and body need occasional periods of absolute rest to recharge mentally, physically or emotionally. During such a time you can store up a reserve of energy in preparation for the next challenge. When the Four of Swords appears in a spread, it suggests such a time is due.

FIVE *of* SWORDS

Element: Air

One man is
*victorious and
holds his swords
high in triumph*

Birds *symbolize
the element of air*

The dark sky is
*ominous in the
background*

The other men
*hang their heads
in defeat*

THEME *Accept the limits of both victory and defeat*

The Five of Swords shows a figure standing in the foreground of the card, holding up three swords in a gesture
of triumph. A further two swords lie crossed at his feet. Behind
him two figures slink away, their heads bowed low in the
shame of defeat. They have surrendered their swords to the

victor and they walk away towards a rough sea and stormy skies. A few birds, reflecting the element of air, can be seen against the darkening sky.

Divinatory Meaning

In the tarot, the number Five always represents some sort of difficulty and tension. In the Five of Swords, the tension is revealed in an image of both victory and defeat which carry their own warnings. One man stands victorious, having successfully defeated two opponents. His opponents have no choice but to hand over their weapons and leave. This card offers a warning against both treachery and deceit, and arrogance in the case of victory.

When this card appears in a reading, it suggests that you may be tackling something that is really too big for you to fight or challenge. The most constructive way of dealing with such situations, whether they occur in the realms of work or personal relationships, is to assess objectively the strength of your opponent relative to your own. Then, if your opponent is much stronger than you, simply turn away. If you are strong enough to acknowledge your opponent's strength and your own weakness, you will not become involved in situations in which you have no hope of victory. The main message of this card is not to take on something that you know secretly will be too much for you. Be prepared to swallow your pride if necessary.

SIX *of* SWORDS

Element: Air

Butterflies reflect the element of air

The black pole symbolizes potential

Rough waters indicate difficult current situation

Calm waters indicate a less challenging time ahead

Dark blue and black shawls represent the air element

THEME *Move away from strife*

The Six of Swords depicts a cloaked boatman rowing two people, wrapped in the dark blue and black shawls of the air element, across a large lake to a hilly shore in the distance. The passengers are both looking around them anxiously as the water they are crossing looks treacherous and rough.

However, ahead of them the water is calm. Six swords stand pointing down into the boat, three behind the boatman and three in front of him and his passengers. The weight of these swords does not appear too heavy for the boat, suggesting that the difficulties of the situation are not too much to bear. The boatman's long pole is black, which symbolizes potential, and he wears a grey tunic with a blue shirt, colours that again reflect the element of air. The sky ahead is clear and a few butterflies fly overhead, once again reflecting the air element linked to the suit of Swords.

Divinatory Meaning

Six is the number of harmony and balance. In the troublesome suit of Swords it indicates a move away from difficult times, signified by the stormy water, towards more peaceful times, symbolized by the calm water ahead. When the Six of Swords appears in a reading, it suggests that there is an opportunity to move out of a difficult situation or relationship, either literally by moving home, job or country, or mentally by using your mind to resolve the complications surrounding you. Perhaps the most encouraging message contained in this card is the idea that it is possible to find an agreeable solution to problems, whether they are physical, mental or emotional. The encouraging aspect of the Six of Swords is that, although you may currently feel burdened with responsibilities, there is calm after the storm on the other side of the water.

SEVEN *of* SWORDS

Element: Air

Cloudy sky shows that the situation is not entirely clear

The man has a surreptitious look, as if leaving without permission

Birds on the flags symbolize the element of air

THEME *A time for tact rather than aggression*

The Seven of Swords shows a man trying to make a sly escape from a military camp. He sneaks away stealthily with seven swords held carefully in both arms. It seems that his departure goes unnoticed by the camp, and his look is one of quiet confidence. The pennants flying from the tent poles display bird motifs, which reflect the airy quality of the suit of Swords. The sky is scattered with little white clouds, again emphasizing the connection between this suit and the element of air. The whole image depicts a carefully thought-out action, which is planned and well executed, rather than something spontaneous, done on emotional impulse.

Divinatory Meaning

The Seven of Swords is an ambivalent card. It suggests a deed that is done in secret, a stealthy and even underhand action, yet it also suggests the use of tact or discretion. A positive interpretation of the Seven of Swords is to remind you of the wisdom of acting cautiously or with diplomacy, to not reveal your hand too readily. For example, if you were to have an idea for a product that might be very popular, it would be unwise to talk about it before it is protected by copyright.

When the Seven of Swords comes up in a reading, it means that you should be careful about being too free and open about your intentions or feelings, as such openness might prove detrimental to you. A less attractive interpretation of this card suggests that you are trying to get away with something dishonourable or even downright dishonest. If this is the case, it can act as a warning of the consequences should you be found out.

EIGHT *of* SWORDS

Element: Air

*The blindfold
signifies her
inability to see
the truth*

*The rope binds
only her arms,
not her legs, so
she is free to
escape*

*The single bird
symbolizes truth*

*The swords are
placed around
her, but there are
spaces between
them for escape*

THEME *Difficulties in becoming free from restriction*

The Eight of Swords shows a blindfolded figure standing in muddy ground, surrounded by eight swords. The blindfold symbolizes a wish not to see things as they really are. The woman is wearing blue robes, connecting the suit of Swords to the element of air, and she has ropes tied around her arms and body. However, her legs are not bound, and, while the swords surround her, they do not actually form a barrier, so although she is restricted, she has the opportunity to leave should she wish to. In the distance atop a high hill sits a castle, which represents authority. The sky is grey and threatening while overhead flies a single bird, emblem of air and symbol of truth.

Divinatory Meaning

Eight is the number of death and regeneration. In the suit of Swords it heralds the end of old or inappropriate ways of thinking and the beginning of something new, symbolized by the bird. However, it can take a while to notice the bird of truth, particularly when you are blindfolded.

When the Eight of Swords appears in a reading, it suggests that you may find yourself in a situation where you feel as though you are 'damned if you do and damned if you don't'. The circumstances in which you find yourself are tricky, and whichever way you turn, you can see disadvantages, so making a choice is not easy. Yet solutions do exist if you can only remove the blindfold and look for them.

This card often conveys a message that a sign of some sort will come your way and suggests that you try to keep an open mind so that you do not miss it. With the Eight of Swords, it feels as though you are imprisoned and restricted from the outside but in fact you are less trapped than you think. However, until you recognize what you have done yourself to create your current situation, you will find it hard to make any changes.

NINE *of* SWORDS

Element: Air

The Swords
do not touch her,
revealing that
her fear is
not based on
external reality

Red hearts and
the motifs of the
air signs of the
zodiac represent
conflict between
feeling and
thinking

Butterflies
symbolize the
element of air

> THEME *Unfounded fears and nightmares*

The Nine of Swords shows an unhappy figure in a pale grey robe. She sits up in bed with her hands covering her face as though she is weeping in fear or anguish. Her bed is carved with a butterfly motif, connecting the card with the element of air, and is covered with a patchwork quilt. The squares on the quilt alternately display red hearts on a blue background and motifs of the air signs of the zodiac – Gemini, Libra and Aquarius – on a white background. This combination of symbols illustrates the conflict between her head and her heart. Nine swords hang over her bed in the dark, pointing down at her but not touching her. The room is otherwise empty.

Divinatory Meaning

Nine is a number in which the forces of the other numbers are gathered together before the final completion in the Ten. The Nine of Swords appears to be an image of enormous gloom: all the troubles in the world seem to be pressing down on the weeping woman. However, none of the swords is actually touching her; they only hang over her in a threatening way.

When the Nine of Swords appears in a reading, it means that the situation may not be as bad as you fear, and that often the fear itself is worse than whatever it is you are afraid of. The Nine of Swords is known as the card of nightmares, but nightmares are not real. The Nine of Swords can also signify that your fears are for loved ones, rather than for yourself. Such fears can leave you feeling impotent because there is nothing you can do about someone else, while you can always find something to do for yourself if you really want to.

The Swords, being the suit of air and the mind, suggest that many of your difficulties are caused by your thoughts, which often do not agree with your feelings. The pattern of zodiacal air signs and red hearts on the quilt symbolizes this conflict clearly, which is certainly a difficult one to solve. It is important to remember, however, that the thing you most fear has not actually happened in the Nine of Swords.

TEN *of* SWORDS

Element: Air

Darkness at the top of the card conveys hopelessness

Ten swords in the man's back symbolize an ending

The butterfly is a symbol of transformation as well as the element of air

Increasing light slowly brings back hope

THEME *The end of a situation or phase*

A figure lies face down on the ground with ten swords piercing his back. It is obvious from the image that something is ending, yet beyond the figure the sea is calm and in the distance the dawn is breaking, symbolizing hope. The sky is very dark at the top of the card, suggesting the absolute loss of hope and direction, yet it slowly lightens towards the moment of dawn, and the light brings back a glimmer of hope. Near the body a single butterfly hovers, symbolizing the element of air and of resurrection.

Divinatory Meaning

The Ten of Swords is undoubtedly a very graphic image of something having ended. The swords have clearly run through the man, and although there is no blood, neither is there much hope of life. However, in the distance the dawn is breaking, as though realization is emerging in consciousness.

When the Ten of Swords appears in a reading, it does signify the end of something, but it does not indicate physical death. The Ten of Swords could refer to the end of a relationship or a job, or to leaving home. It also indicates that the change occurs because whatever has been operating is no longer valid. This card may also reflect change and endings in terms of your attitudes, and often brings with it a ring of truth. We may refuse to see things the way they really are simply because we prefer our illusions and wish to preserve them. The Ten of Swords tends to put a rather abrupt end to such pretence and shows us life as it really is 'in the cold light of day'. While it is often painful when our self-made illusions are stripped away, it also provides an opportunity for something real and truthful to grow in the place of falsity.

PAGE *of* SWORDS

Element: Air

The tilt of the sword to the left suggests the creative power of the mind

Birds symbolize the element of air

The Page's youth represents new beginnings in the thought process

Butterflies symbolize the element of air

THEME *New beginnings in mental activity*

The Page of Swords shows a young boy, wearing a blue tunic and a white shirt, reflecting the colours of the sky. The shirt is trimmed with butterflies to connect the figure with the element of air. He is holding up a sword with both hands, which he tilts to the left of the card, the side of creativity. He is alert and ready to guard himself against attack. The Page of Swords is an image of the versatility and creativity of the mind. Above him fly several birds, symbolizing the mind's ability to soar high above mundane reality and hold several different thoughts together at once.

Divinatory Meaning

The Pages of the tarot are all depicted as youthful, and in the airy suit of Swords the young boy represents new and as yet unformed ideas. In order to learn, it is necessary to experiment with thoughts and concepts as well as discuss them with others. The Page of Swords has a reputation for being at best mischievous and at worst malicious. The element of air is in its least developed form in this card, and the Page of Swords can represent a person who tends towards gossip and idle chat rather than verbal exchanges that are profitable and truly informative. Children and adolescents chatter and gossip as a way of learning how to interact with each other and, although the discussions may not seem deep, they are nevertheless an important stage that must be passed through before attaining more profound levels of interaction.

When the Page of Swords appears in a reading, it can indicate the first stages of a relationship, which starts as mundane chatter but may well develop into something more meaningful in time. It may also represent the inner stirrings of an idea that needs to be given time and attention if it is to gain momentum and reach maturity.

KNIGHT *of* SWORDS

Element: Air

The horse and rider almost fly along, giving the impression of extreme speed

The horse's bridle is decorated with birds – a symbol of air

The trees bend back in the wind, which is symbolic of the power of the airy element

THEME *Welcome change that might be disruptive*

A dashing young man is riding on a racing grey horse whose mane flies out in the wind and whose legs are outstretched. The emphasis of this image is speed. The Knight holds his sword straight out ahead of him. Clouds scud across the skies, while trees in the background bend with the strong wind. His horse's bridle is decorated with birds and he wears a blue cloak that flies in the wind. His silver helmet is open to show his face, and a long white feather flies from the top of it.

Divinatory Meaning

The Knight of Swords, like the other Knights of the tarot, appears on horseback. The Knights are depicted in motion because they are all on their own particular quest. The Knight of Swords is on a quest for knowledge and information, not necessarily for deep wisdom, but more for its own sake. The emphasis is on speed and gathering information as quickly as possible rather than as deeply as possible.

The Knight of Swords is connected with Gemini, the sign of the zodiac associated with the acquisition of knowledge and communication. Geminis love to talk and to think about obscure or interesting things but, like the butterfly, they only pause for an instant to gather nectar from a flower before moving off again, seeking another potentially more interesting flower to sip from. The Gemini personality is stimulating and fun but easily bored. Similarly, the Knight of Swords has the reputation for rushing into things, be it people's lives, affections or work, turning them upside down and then leaving.

In a reading, the Knight of Swords may represent an actual person who enters your life, bringing with him or her a somewhat chaotic influence before moving swiftly on. This may not be as bad as it sounds because it is quite possible that you need such an influence in order to shake up the status quo. Alternatively, this card might suggest that you are wishing to develop your mind in some way. This may come into effect through a course of study or a change of career.

QUEEN *of* SWORDS

Element: Air

Clear skies indicate her potential to rise above her sorrow

The bird represents her single-minded clarity of vision

Storm clouds indicate sorrow

Her cloak reflects the sky, which is a symbol of the element of air

Her throne is decorated with an angel: spirit of the air

THEME *Suffering with dignity and resignation*

The Queen of Swords is a dignified, solemn-looking woman who sits facing towards the left, which is the side of creativity and experience. She holds her sword bolt upright as a symbol of justice. Storm clouds gather around her in the lower part of the sky, while the sky above her head is clear blue, symbolizing that she is able to keep her head high even when difficulties surround her. A single bird flies above her as a symbol of her clarity of vision. Her stone throne is carved with an angel of the spirit and butterflies, and her cloak is like a blue sky full of white clouds. All these motifs represent the element of air.

Divinatory Meaning

The noble Queen of Swords is often connected with the serious or sorrowful side of the suit of Swords. She is commonly known as one who suffers; one who has known pain yet bears her suffering with dignity. The Queen of Swords would bear any upset she may feel with courage and fortitude rather than wear her heart on her sleeve like the Queen of Cups.

The Queen of Swords is linked with Aquarius and those born under this sign are known to keep their feelings well hidden, although they are perfectly friendly and polite. All the air signs, which are closely linked with the suit of Swords, lay a strong emphasis on being civilized and even cool rather than risk ugly emotional scenes. The air signs, and Aquarius is no exception, have high ideals and expectations of life, love and friendship, and as a consequence feel disappointed and discouraged when reality so often falls short of their dreams.

If the Queen of Swords appears in a reading, it suggests that a courageous, idealistic, yet possibly aloof person may enter your life; one who is determined to accept whatever difficulties arise without showing fear or dismay. Alternatively, the appearance of this card may mean that you need to develop such qualities within yourself.

KING *of* SWORDS

Element: Air

Two birds indicate the duality of his thoughts

Butterflies are a reflection of the element of air

His sword is tilted to his right, the side of action

His cloak is purple, the colour of wisdom

THEME *An authority figure, firm but fair*

The King of Swords depicts an upright man with a serious expression. He wears a blue robe, reflecting the element of air, and a cloak of purple, the colour of wisdom. He faces straight ahead, and holds his sword upright, yet not straight up for pure wisdom, but tilted slightly to his right, the side of action. He sits on a throne of stone, carved with butterflies, symbols of the element of air. His expression is calm and dignified for he takes his position of authority seriously. Above his head two birds fly: a bird symbolizes the mind's ability to rise high above the realm of ordinary mortals, and Two is the number of choice and balance. The King of Swords, while seeking truth, realizes that it cannot exist in perfect form.

Divinatory Meaning

The King of Swords is an authority figure, representing just laws and social harmony. He has a fine mind, which he uses to seek out fair solutions. The King of Swords prizes intellectual ability highly and considers the development of mental achievements a priority.

Traditionally, the King of Swords is associated with the legal profession as a way of implementing truth and social justice. Astrologically, he is connected with Libra, the zodiacal sign concerned with harmony and balance. The scales of Libra have to be adjusted constantly if life is to remain in an equitable state, and the King of Swords is prepared to try to achieve such a balance. As a character he is charming, polite and well mannered, yet his mind is sharp and he can be quite ruthless. Librans like to preserve an outward appearance of calm and order, which can in reality conceal inner turmoil.

If the King of Swords appears in a reading, it could be that someone enters your life who embodies the qualities of this shrewd yet charming King; someone who outwits his opponents through the clever use of words rather than brute force. Alternatively, it might indicate that you need to develop some of these qualities in yourself.

Sample Reading for Swords

*M*ary, a middle-aged mother, came to see me about her feelings regarding her teenage twins, a son and a daughter, who were both leaving home at the same time. She chose the following five cards from the suit of Swords.

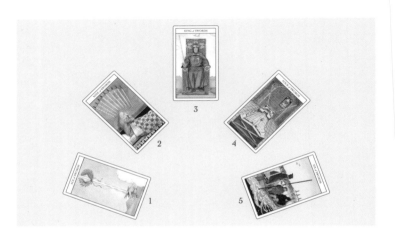

1. Present Position: Ace of Swords

The Aces signify new beginnings, and the Ace of Swords suggests that out of a difficult situation something new and positive can begin to emerge. Mary needed to come to terms with the end of a phase in her life in which she was identified solely as a mother, and to see that life might have something else to offer.

2. Present Expectations: Nine of Swords

The Nine of Swords represents fears and feelings of doom, which do not actually have any bearing on reality. The card of nightmares does not mean that awful events will actually happen. It indicates that Mary fears how she is going to feel once her son and daughter have left home rather than how she actually will feel.

3. What is Unexpected: King of Swords

The King of Swords is a card of authority and signifies an ability to use the mind well. It could mean that Mary will, in fact, take charge of her life in a new way, and find opportunities to use her intellectual capability to a positive effect.

4. Immediate Future: Four of Swords

The Four of Swords is a card of rest and recuperation. It can be seen as a time of recovery. In Mary's case it suggests a time of coming to terms with the new situation in the home: a time of calm and reflection. She will also need to allow some time to grieve when the moment of separation arrives.

5. Long-term Future: Six of Swords

The Six of Swords suggests moving away from a turbulent and possibly unhappy period towards something calmer and clearer. Mary was able to take hope that her life would not end after the children had left home, and could begin to imagine that something meaningful would gradually emerge to fill the void.

Conclusion

Mary was experiencing a very big change in her life (Ace of Swords) and was very frightened about how it would affect her (Nine of Swords). She did not initially expect to be able to find the mental strength to cope with this change (King of Swords). She needed to allow herself a period of withdrawal to adjust to her new life (Four of Swords) before finding a positive direction to follow (Six of Swords).

ACE *of* PENTACLES

Element: Earth

The open arch symbolizes the freedom to move on

The border hedge represents a container

Red roses symbolize passion

The beautiful garden shows nature's bounty

White lilies symbolize the spirit

THEME *A gift or financial opportunity*

On the Ace of Pentacles, a magical hand appears from a cloud, offering up a large gold pentacle held in its palm. The suit of Pentacles belongs to the element of earth, which, like the watery Cups, is feminine and creative in an obvious way. Unlike the fiery Wands or the airy Swords, which are

outgoing and masculine in their creativity, the Pentacles draw
on the wisdom of the earth and the body to perform their function. Beneath the hand is a garden full of red roses, symbolic of
passion and desire, mixed with white lilies, which represent the
spirit, alongside other vegetation, symbolizing the richness of
the earth's bounty. The garden is enclosed by a hedge, indicating the need for a safe container in which to learn the lessons
of the Pentacles. Yet an archway leads out into open countryside, suggesting the freedom to move once the lesson is
learned. The image is peaceful and fruitful, and suggests
abundance.

Divinatory Meaning

The Ace of Pentacles, like all the Aces, indicates an opportunity for a new start. In the case of the earthy Pentacles, the
new energy that emerges is often connected with financial or
material matters. It may take the obvious form of a financial
gift that appears like 'magic' or as a result of 'good luck', or it
can take the form of a successful dividend earned through
sheer hard work. Either way, something is about to be made
concrete through the spark of inspiration created by the Ace.

When it appears in a reading, the Ace of Pentacles may
indicate that you are ready to invest the energy and drive
required to found a new business, or to start a promising new
career or employment. The Ace of Pentacles signifies the
possibilities of material achievement because there is a real
desire to put in the essential hard work. The initial idea or
encouragement for a project may arrive like a magical hand
from the sky, but the lush garden is only possible as a result of
patient, persistent and consistent hard work.

TWO *of* PENTACLES

Element: Earth

Two pentacles fly up in the air, symbolizing fluctuating finances

Two ships represent the figure's fortunes

The mouse is a symbol of the earth

THEME *Change and versatility*

The Two of Pentacles depicts a juggler dressed in simple clothes. The green and brown of his clothes reflect the colours of the earthy element. He throws two gold pentacles up into the air as if hoping to catch them both as they fall. Behind him two ships, representing his fortunes, are navigating their route through rough but not overly dangerous seas. The image reveals that a juggling of money matters is required, but, although the situation carries a certain tension, it is not unduly alarming. The figure is standing on a level grassy verge, which symbolizes a solid base and indicates potential. A little mouse can be seen in the bottom right-hand corner of the card, reinforcing the earth element.

Divinatory Meaning

The Two of Pentacles is a card of action, movement and change. The image is of a juggler who must keep two balls in the air, signifying the need to pay attention to several things at once. As the Pentacles are the suit of the earth element – reflected in the image by the earthy colours and the little mouse – the juggled items are most likely to be connected with material and financial issues.

When this card appears in reading, it can mean that you will face some fluctuation and change materially, although this is not necessarily negative. On the contrary, it may point towards quite creative solutions to material problems. However, as nothing is quite certain financially when the Two of Pentacles appears, it may mean that you will have to 'borrow from Peter to pay back Paul'. Nevertheless, on the whole, the enthusiasm engendered through this card tends to override any oscillation that its appearance may also suggest.

THREE *of* PENTACLES

Element: Earth

The scaffold shows the building is unfinished

The yellow robe represents mental energy

The three pentacles in place represent what has already been achieved

The mallet symbolizes the work that still needs to be done

THEME *Initial completion of work*

The Three of Pentacles depicts a workman leaving a building that has reached the first stage of completion. The workman is dressed in the brown and green colours symbolic of the earth element. The image would seem to suggest that the workman has been discussing plans for the building with the couple dressed in robes of yellow and orange, signifying mental energy. When constructing a building, knowledge and experience are required, as well as practical skill, which is demonstrated by the earth element of this card. The three people stand in the interior of a grand property with a solid structure, which is yet unfinished. Three pentacles are carved into the wall of the staircase along with foliage and vines, which symbolize the element of earth. A little mouse, another symbol of the earthy element, is scurrying down the stairs.

Divinatory Meaning

The Three of Pentacles combines the initial completion of the Three with the earthy nature of the Pentacles. This card suggests that a certain level of achievement has been reached. Yet the building is not yet finished; indeed, there is still a long way to go before completion.

When the Three of Pentacles comes up in a reading, it suggests that concrete progress has been attained, perhaps in work or in establishing something solid in home life. This could take the form of buying a house: you have acquired the basic structure but the decoration or renovation is still to be done. This card suggests that the basic structure is sound and only the finer details have yet to be carried out.

There is a double-edged aspect that applies to some extent to all the Threes: there is satisfaction for having reached the first stage coupled with frustration that the project still has a long way to go before it is finished. As an earthy suit, the Pentacles are particularly concerned with anything connected with the material world, so this card can indicate slow but steady progress in business matters.

FOUR *of* PENTACLES

Element: Earth

The figure holds on tightly to his golden pentacle, indicating a miserly nature

The brick wall separates him emotionally from the people of the city beyond

Rich clothes represent his love of material goodness

Sitting on the trunk indicates his fear of being robbed

THEME *Holding on too tightly*

The Four of Pentacles shows a richly dressed man sitting firmly on a trunk decorated with three pentacles, while he holds on to a fourth in rather a desperate way. His fine clothes indicate his value for material possessions, as does the way he clutches the fourth pentacle closely to his heart as if gold is what he most desires. He sits firmly on the chest, which the three pentacles on the side suggest contains money, so that nothing may escape from the trunk, nor may anyone steal anything from it. The man seems disconnected from the city beyond, cut off by a brick wall, which separates him from other people. A little mouse, a reminder of the element of earth, creeps past the trunk.

Divinatory Meaning

Four is the number that represents the material world and, in the earthy suit of Pentacles, it suggests a strong commitment to financial and business matters. The Four of Pentacles has the reputation of being the card of the miser, as it can symbolize a great fear and suspicion of parting with financial assets or material goods. There may be great reluctance to let go of money or worldly position, and while this means that nothing is lost, it also means that nothing is achieved either. This situation results in the flow of energy being stifled, so at best nothing changes and at worst things stagnate.

If this card appears in a reading, it suggests that an overwhelming desire for material security and stability may hinder your ability to expand and grow because of the exaggerated fear of taking material risks. As your attitude to money can also be reflected in the way you react emotionally, the Four of Pentacles can also suggest that there could be fear and dread of loss. It is possible that there is anxiety about being too free with your feelings for fear of emotional hurt.

FIVE *of* PENTACLES

Element: Earth

The presence of a church, a place of spiritual worship, indicates possible loss of spiritual faith or meaning

The destitute beggars symbolize material loss

The mouse indicates the element of earth

THEME *Loss of wealth or faith*

The Five of Pentacles depicts a brightly lit stained-glass window, which looks as though it belongs to a church, representing a place of sanctuary, both physically and spiritually. In the window, five shining pentacles are surrounded by coloured fruit and flowers, which are symbols of the earth element of this suit. However, outside the church the weather is cold and the normally fertile earth does not yield any of its bounty as it is covered by a layer of snow. Two ragged beggars, one on crutches, shelter beneath the window, but they do not look up towards the warm interior. They are lost in their own misfortune and misery and do not appear to notice that help is, in fact, nearby. The Five of Pentacles emphasizes the loss of material possessions rather than the bounty of the earth. A mouse in the corner of the card reminds us of the essential earthy nature of the suit of Pentacles.

Divinatory Meaning

Five is a number that generally augurs anxiety and tension in all the four suits. In the earthy suit of Pentacles it can suggest that the difficulties may be of a financial nature, although this is by no means the only significance of this card. We often measure self-worth by material status, so if that material status takes a dive, so does our sense of personal value. Notice that the beggars do not look up towards the lighted window. This indicates that a more serious problem might be a lack of faith in yourself as well as a low sense of self-esteem.

The underlying message of the Five of Pentacles is that not only may there be difficulty in holding on to finances, but more importantly, you may be in danger of losing a sense of belief in the goodness or meaning of life. When this card appears in a reading, it would be advisable to pay great attention to both the material and spiritual areas of life.

Six *of* Pentacles

Element: Earth

The castle is a symbol of wealth and stability

The scales represent fortune balanced out carefully

The mouse is a symbol of the element of earth

The vine leaves on the arch represent earth's riches

THEME *Generosity and charity*

The Six of Pentacles shows a well-dressed man offering alms to the poor. Two beggars, both wearing brown-coloured robes, which are appropriate to the earth element of this suit, hold out their hands, while their benefactor counts out coins into the palm of one. The wealthy man holds a set of balanced scales in his left hand, the passive side, and uses his right hand, the active side, to distribute the money. The image is one of charity and benevolence. Above, a fine stone arch represents stability and permanence. Six pentacles are carved out of the stone along with vine leaves, symbols of the bounty of the earth. In the distance lies a castle, symbol of wealth and good fortune. A little mouse on the ledge of the arch is the familiar symbol of the element of earth.

Divinatory Meaning

Six is the number of balance and equality. In the suit of Pentacles it indicates the need to share wealth and good fortune. The image on the card shows a rich man giving aid to those less materially successful, suggesting that monetary aid will be available when necessary. Another deeper meaning can also be read into this card: emotional as well as physical aid may either be offered or received.

When this card appears in a reading, this benevolence can either be given by you to others in greater need, or received by you from others. The essential message of this card is the idea that you give when you can and take when you must. In life no one will ever always be in the offering role, nor always in the receiving; we will all have opportunities to give and to take. The fact that the man holds a set of scales is significant: he is measuring out exactly what is needed, no more and no less. When the Six of Pentacles comes up in a reading you will find yourself in a position of receiving or giving what you need, which may not be the same as what you want.

SEVEN *of* PENTACLES

Element: Earth

The well-established pentacles represent what has been achieved already

The single pentacle represents what could be achieved if the man changes direction

The rabbit is a symbol of the earth element

THEME *The need to decide*

The Seven of Pentacles depicts a man dressed in the green and brown that symbolize the element of earth. He stands between two fields: the one on his right shows a well-established crop with six pentacles appearing to flourish in its midst. To his left the crop is less developed and a single pentacle stands alone as if indicating the promise of something new and not yet rooted. The man cannot decide whether to continue with the established crop on his right or pursue the new direction on his left. His surroundings also remind us of the element of earth with rich healthy crops and a rabbit, symbol of fertility, darting across the path behind him.

Divinatory Meaning

Seven is the number relating to knowledge, and the Seven of Pentacles is a card that symbolizes the need to make a decision. The man in the image has clearly achieved much with his fine crop of six pentacles on the left of the card, the side of creativity and passivity. However, the single pentacle on the right, the side of activity, suggests that a new avenue or opportunity could be opening up.

When this card appears in a reading, it usually points towards a choice between two paths of action. One path is familiar, tried, tested and known to be profitable, while the other path suggests something altogether new and even alien. This card does not make any kind of judgement as to which is the 'right' path. It merely illustrates that it is time to direct energy towards one side or another, and it is up to you to make that choice. There are likely to be advantages and disadvantages to either course, and it is up to you to weigh each up and act accordingly.

EIGHT *of* PENTACLES

Element: Earth

The workshop symbolizes a place of industry

The field and orchards suggest nature's goodness

The man is measuring carefully to show his intention of getting his work right

The mouse symbolizes the earth element

THEME *Learning new skills*

The Eight of Pentacles depicts a young workman, who wears his apprentice apron and cap with pleasure, busy in his workshop. He carves out a pentacle on a bench with care and precision. On the board behind him seven completed pentacles are nailed up. Small sprigs of grass grow on the workshop floor, suggesting new ideas, while outside fields and orchards can be glimpsed, symbolizing the bounty of the earth. A small mouse, symbol of the earth element, hides under the table. The scene is one of industry and talent.

Divinatory Meaning

Eight is the number of regeneration, and in the suit of Pentacles it suggests a new direction in your career. It is known as the card of the apprentice because it often denotes a change in direction, which may involve training or study. Training for mature students is generally a far greater pleasure than for schoolchildren as the course of study is chosen rather than required. Consequently, the worker in the image appears busy and contented. He clearly finds his work absorbing, and a genuine source of interest and pleasure. This card signifies both skill and the discipline required to excel in the work. The earthy suit of Pentacles describes our attitude towards the material side of life: it seems generally accepted that people are happier when they are paid for their work, rather than when they must work only for pay.

When the Eight of Pentacles appears in a reading, it offers an opportunity to follow a direction, even if it means under- taking a course of training or study, which truly inspires you. Although the worker in the image is lost in his own private world of work, the door to his workshop is open, connecting him to the outside world from which he will ultimately receive his rewards and accolades.

NINE *of* PENTACLES

Element: Earth

The hunting bird represents her far-reaching intellect and imagination

The castle is an image of material stability and security

The vines symbolize the riches of the earth

The woman is well-dressed to symbolize her material success

The rabbit is a symbol of fertility and fecundity

THEME *Success and enjoyment*

The Nine of Pentacles depicts a finely dressed woman whose beautiful robes are decorated with flowers. She stands in a rich and fertile vineyard, and twines her fingers into the vine with her left hand. The vines symbolize the earth's generosity, which she is able to appreciate and enjoy. In her right hand she holds a falcon, a hunting bird, which represents her far-reaching intellect and imagination. The nine pentacles are incorporated into the abundance of fruit and foliage that surrounds her, and she appears contented with her lot. Beside her is a rabbit, the symbol of earthy fertility. In the far distance a castle stands at the top of a hill, a symbol of her achievements and high aspirations as well as material stability and security.

Divinatory Meaning

Nine is the number in which all the other numbers combine to form a foundation before the completion of the cycle in the Ten. The Nine of Pentacles depicts material security and comfort. The woman in the image is beautifully dressed, calm and contented. She is surrounded by the riches of the earth: having worked to achieve success, she is now able to enjoy the good things in life.

The woman is alone in the image, except for her bird, which symbolizes the power of thought and imagination. She does not need other people, which does not mean she does not want them, nor does it mean that she will not have them. It simply means that she has reached a point of contentment within herself at a deep level that allows her to feel quite happy even if she finds herself alone. She is able to be proud of her achievements and at peace with herself and as such has no need of an audience to tell her she has done well. When this card appears in a reading, it suggests a calm period during which you can fully appreciate the positive in your life and enjoy a sense of harmony with the world about you.

TEN *of* PENTACLES

Element: Earth

The castle is an image of security and stability passed down through generations

The old man, daughter and child represent the family tradition

The dog is a symbol of the earth element

THEME *The passing on of positive traditions*

The Ten of Pentacles depicts a family group, comprising a grandfather with his grandchild on his knee and his daughter by his side, enjoying the tranquillity and beauty of their well-established garden. In the distance stands a fine castle, symbol of a long-held family tradition. As castles were commonly passed down through the family, it also represents security and stability in a fast-changing world. The family dog appears in this card, both as an image of loyalty and of the natural world, as does the richness of the flourishing garden, another symbol of the earth element of the suit of Pentacles.

Divinatory Meaning

Ten is the number of completion, and in the Pentacles it points towards completion and continuation in one. The image is one that describes a family tradition, founded though hard work and commitment to a common purpose. The element of earth is perhaps the most attuned to the notion of 'as you sow, so shall you reap'. A key message of the Ten of Pentacles is that you must be prepared to invest time and energy both financially and emotionally in order to gain in the longer term, rather than expecting to receive a rich harvest without planting a single seed.

When the Ten of Pentacles appears in a reading, it means that something needs to be made concrete for the future. It may indicate that it is the right time to buy a home, start a family or put something substantial in place for the future. This could mean passing on family traditions in a positive way, or it could indicate inheritance or gifts of a material nature, or the less tangible gifts of love and support offered by the family. An important aspect of the Ten of Pentacles is making something manifest that will live on after you have gone. Naturally, this may refer to the creation of children but it can also refer to areas of research or artistic or literary creations, which can continue to benefit future generations, long after their creator has ceased to exist.

PAGE *of* PENTACLES

Element: Earth

Robes are brown
and green,
symbolizing the
earth element

The rabbit
represents
fertility and
fecundity

New crop
appearing
indicates new
beginnings

THEME *Small beginnings*

All the Pages are symbolic of youthful potential as yet unfulfilled. The Page of Pentacles depicts a young boy wearing simple robes of earthy browns and greens. He stands in a ploughed field where the new sprouts of a fresh crop peep through the earth. This is an image of new beginnings as indicated by the new crop, which also suggests that nature unfolds in its own time and cannot be hurried. The young man holds a single pentacle carefully in both hands, as if aware of its unique potential. A rabbit, symbol of fertility and fecundity, scampers freely in the field behind him.

Divinatory Meaning

The Pages, as we have seen in the other suits, represent ideas or projects in their infancy or early stages. So, the Page of Pentacles refers to the making of something large and concrete out of a small, seemingly insignificant, beginning. The traditional meaning of this card is that an opportunity for material success exists, which may start out on a small scale but which eventually will grow into something quite substantial. The Page of Pentacles represents the beginning of this process and his appearance in a reading reminds us of the necessity of laying firm foundations at the base of any new venture to enable it to grow into something important. The Page of Pentacles is associated with hard work and diligence.

When this card appears in a reading, it may point to the arrival in your life of a serious and thoughtful person who either helps you to found something or perhaps sets you a good example in making careful plans for the beginning of a project. Alternatively, this card may indicate that the time is ripe for you to develop something in yourself.

KNIGHT *of* PENTACLES

Element: Earth

Oak leaves represent the slow growth and progress from acorn to mighty oak

The Knight's carthorse is built for work, not speed

The field mouse symbolizes the earth element

THEME *Progress is slow but steady*

The Knight of Pentacles shows a young man dressed as a Knight, with an over-tunic embroidered with oak leaves, sitting astride a carthorse which stands still in the middle of a recently ploughed field. He is holding a pentacle. There are richer crops in the background and the scene depicts the natural cycles of birth, blossom and decay so central to the earthy nature of the suit of Pentacles. Decorative oak leaves adorn his helmet rather than the flamboyant feathers worn by the other Knights, highlighting his connection with the element of earth, as does the field mouse standing in the furrows.

Divinatory Meaning

The Knight of Pentacles is depicted standing motionless in a ploughed field. Unlike the Knights of the other suits, the Knight of Pentacles is the only one who is seated on a carthorse, and his mount is the only one that is stationary. The other Knights symbolize action and movement, while the Knight of Pentacles represents gradual progress. His horse is designed for hard work rather than speed or style. He is a symbol of patience and perseverance; he is not extravagant nor easily knocked off course. The great strength of the Knight of Pentacles is that he will accomplish what he sets out to do simply by following the course absolutely and painstakingly. Although he may be accused of being boring, he always achieves his goals.

The Knight of Pentacles is connected with the earth sign of Virgo, a sign known for its fastidiousness and keen attention to detail. In a reading, the Knight of Pentacles may indicate that a person who has the qualities of kindness, reliability and honesty is about to enter your life. It may also mean that you need to develop these qualities in yourself, or you may need to be patient in assisting a matter slowly to its proper conclusion.

QUEEN *of* PENTACLES

Element: Earth

Roses are a symbol of beauty and love

The bulls' heads are a symbol of Taurus

The garden is a symbol of the fruits of the earth

The rabbit is a symbol of fertility

THEME *Love of luxury*

The Queen of Pentacles is depicted sitting on a stone throne richly carved with bulls' heads. The bull symbolizes the earth sign Taurus with which the Queen of Pentacles is connected. The fruits of the earth also adorn the throne, which stands in a lush garden, indicating nature's abundance.

Among the various flowers that grow in the garden are some roses, and rose motifs also decorate the Queen's cloak. Roses are a symbol of youth and beauty, and are especially connected with Venus, the ruling planet of Taurus. A rabbit sits by the throne as a sign of fertility. The Queen holds a pentacle, symbol of nature's magic, on her lap and looks at it lovingly.

Divinatory Meaning

The Queen of Pentacles represents a person who is practical and materialistic, both aware of and in touch with the real world. She is connected with earthy reality in a way that the Queens of the other suits are not. The suit of Pentacles is harnessed to the earth in a very matter-of-fact way. The Queen of Pentacles is fully aware of herself as a sensual being who values the body and its needs in an unashamed way. She is quite ready and willing to work hard for what she wants, and is equally content to enjoy the fruits of her labours. Like those born under the sign of Taurus, which is connected with this card, the Queen of Pentacles enjoys the pleasure of good food, fine wine and beauty in her clothes and surroundings. She is generous, both towards herself and towards others, giving of her best both emotionally and practically.

If this card appears in a reading, it might be that a person who possesses the qualities of the earthy Queen is about to enter your life. Alternatively, it might be that this is a time during which you need to pay extra attention to your physical needs and indulge your sensual wants.

KING *of* PENTACLES

Element: Earth

Grapes
*symbolize the
sweetness of
the earth*

*The castle
represents wealth
and status*

*The mountain
goat is a symbol
of Capricorn*

THEME *Financial security and stability*

The King of Pentacles is depicted in rich robes decorated with grapes and vine leaves. A real vine grows either side of him. The vines symbolize the wealth of the earth, and the grapes its sweetness. His stone throne is carved with goats' heads, the mountain goat being the symbol of Capricorn, the sign of the zodiac with which the King of Pentacles is connected. He holds an orb in his left hand as a symbol of temporal power, and a pentacle in his right, as a symbol of the earth's magic. Behind him stands an impressive castle, which represents his earthly achievements and material possessions.

Divinatory Meaning

The King of Pentacles appears as a figure of majesty and authority. He is an image of human ambition, which resonates with the sign of Capricorn, and represents a wish for status and the power that status gives. The King of Pentacles describes someone who has worked hard for success and is pleased with the achievement. Like the Queen of Pentacles, he is determined to enjoy and benefit from his worldly goods. Like all the earth Court cards, the King of Pentacles is well aware of the necessity for effort and labour in order to achieve. He is not afraid of hard work and is, as a consequence, able to reap what he sows with calm appreciation. Capricorn is the sign of worldly position, and the King of Pentacles desires respect and status. The strong sense of determination and wish to succeed generally leads Capricorn to the longed-for goal, be it wealth, power or social status.

When this card appears in a reading, it suggests that either a powerful figure like the King of Pentacles will enter your life, or that you may need to develop his qualities of ambition and determination yourself to succeed materially and socially. While the King of Pentacles may not have the more colourfully dynamic qualities of the other Kings, he is a very strong character with a generous nature and high moral principles.

Sample Reading for Pentacles

*J*ames, a forty-year-old family man, came to see me to ask how his situation would look financially if he were to change his working direction. He chose the following five cards from the suit of Pentacles.

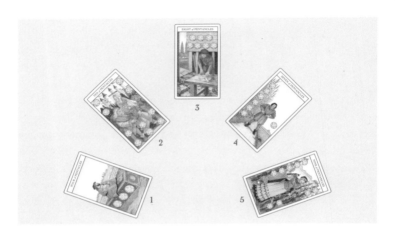

1. Present Position: Four of Pentacles

The Four of Pentacles is a card that indicates fear of taking a risk, and fear of letting go of money or control. James admitted that he was very nervous about leaving his current job, which was financially secure but did not satisfy him creatively at all.

2. Present Expectations: Ten of Pentacles

This card suggests stability and security. The Ten of Pentacles often refers to property and family money. James said that most of his money was tied up in his large home and if he were to branch out into another direction he would need to sell the house to realize some capital.

3. *What is Unexpected: Eight of Pentacles*

This card suggests a training or apprenticeship. In James's case it seemed to indicate the possibility of a new start that would involve learning a new skill or using an existing talent in a different way.

4. *Immediate Future: Seven of Pentacles*

This card indicates a difficult decision between something that is well established and known, and something unknown and untried. James said that this described his dilemma perfectly as he was keen to leave his lucrative but soul-destroying job in a bank and follow his long-held dream to run his own restaurant but was afraid of the potentially negative effect such a move would have on the whole family.

5. *Long-term Future: Nine of Pentacles*

The Nine of Pentacles indicates material comfort and stability coupled with a sense of satisfaction that one's own efforts have produced this lifestyle. It was unclear whether this would come from his current secure position or from taking a new career direction.

Conclusion

James needed to let go financially and emotionally (Four of Pentacles). This did not necessarily mean that he should take 'the big risk' but he could learn to be less rigid inside. He was comfortable and secure (Ten of Pentacles), and could be grateful that he could at least choose to change his working life if he wished. He should be aware that a move would involve further training (Eight of Pentacles). Perhaps he might consider undertaking training while still in his current job. He has a lot of consider (Seven of Pentacles), yet seems to have a secure outlook for the moment (Nine of Pentacles).

Sample Reading for Minor Arcana

W*e will now combine all the suits in a reading. When you try this, you will notice that the reading becomes more complex but also more interesting and challenging. The following sample reading uses the fifty-six cards of the Minor Arcana in a traditional spread called the Celtic Cross. Such a spread is particularly good for gaining a general impression of a person's situation in everyday terms.*

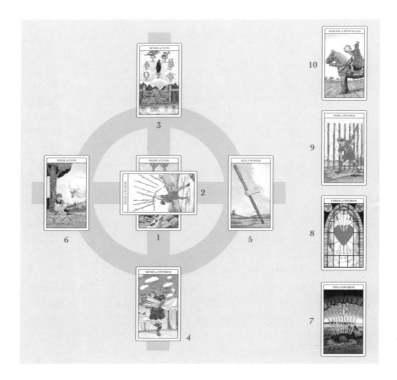

I like to do a structured reading, using a combination of three spreads to build up a complete picture of the person's situation. I start with the Celtic Cross spread, using only the cards of the Minor Arcana to explore the details of the subject's circumstances at an everyday level. I follow this with the Star spread, using only the cards of the Major Arcana to explore what is going on within the psyche of the person – their inner life (see pages 186–8). Finally, for an overall summary of the situation, I join the Major and Minor Arcanas together and lay out the Horseshoe spread (see pages 189–91).

Catherine, a woman in her thirties, came to see me to talk about her future direction. Although she said she did not have a real 'problem', there were nevertheless issues arising surrounding career and family life that she wanted to discuss. She was married with two young children but also ran her own business from home. Although this provided just enough income together with flexibility regarding childcare, Catherine was beginning to miss the stimulation and sociability of a busy office environment. At the same time, her husband was quite keen to move out of the city and live a simpler life. Catherine was not sure how well suited she would be to a country existence.

Catherine selected ten cards from the Minor Arcana, and I laid them out in the Celtic Cross spread as follows:

1. Present Position: Eight of Cups

This card indicates the need to leave behind a situation even though a great deal of care and energy has been invested in it. Notice the figure turning his back on the carefully stacked cups as he heads towards the barren hills. Catherine felt this referred to her situation, regarding working from home. The business she ran was very time-consuming, not always as interesting as she wished it to be and did not bring in enough money to make it seem worth the stress involved. Catherine felt that if it were either more stimulating creatively or made a great deal of money, it would be worth the effort. However, as the business did not fulfil either criteria she wished she could find an alternative way of working which would provide the stimulation missing from the current situation.

2. What Crosses You: Eight of Wands

The second card describes the obstacles that currently face Catherine. The Eight of Wands is a card of energy, creativity and ideas, suggesting a time for positive action. Because the card is in the position of What crosses you, it means that, although activity is possible, it is delayed or frustrated in some way. Catherine felt that her life was so tightly structured that she did not have enough time or space to explore the new avenues represented by the Eight of Wands.

3. What is Above You: Seven of Cups

The third card indicates that ideas are currently 'in the air' but nothing is actually happening. The image on the card reveals a rich array of options but they remain engulfed in clouds and have not been translated into reality. The Seven of Cups did, Catherine felt, describe accurately how she was feeling: lots of fanciful notions, many wishes but nothing concrete. She needed to pick one idea to focus on so that she could gradually turn that dream into a reality.

4. What is Beneath You: Seven of Swords

The fourth card suggests the need to keep things 'close to your chest'. Notice the stealthy way in which the man escapes from the camp, clutching his seven swords tightly. Indeed, Catherine felt that this reflected the way she had begun to avoid discussing her ideas of possible ways forward with her husband. He was actually quite happy with the ways things were and, apart from relocating the family to the country, did not want anything to change. He worked from home too and liked the flexibility of their sharing the working and domestic duties. Whenever Catherine had suggested pursuing her career outside the home, he had become upset, raising all sorts of objections generally concerning income and the stress for everyone if she were to be away from the home, working long days.

5. *What is Behind You: Ace of Wands*

The fifth card reflects the recent past. The creative start that the Ace of Wands suggests was certainly in evidence when Catherine left her prestigious job in the city and started her business from home. She had at that time been very excited about combining her working life with her new domestic life, but her enthusiasm had begun to wane more recently, as she had become bored by the routine and lack of social contact. At the same time, she could not see a way of developing the business further – to take it to a new phase – without changing the set up completely, involving risk and increased stress levels.

6. *What is Before You: Four of Cups*

The Four of Cups shows a figure with three cups in front of him and another offered from the clouds, yet he sits with arms folded, looking glum. The Four of Cups is the card of discontent despite having many blessings. Catherine was quite aware of the fact that in many ways her life worked very well and she had much to be grateful for. She identified strongly with the figure on the card, for, although she knew she was in many ways fortunate, she still felt dissatisfied. She felt frustrated in her desire to change the pattern of her working life, seeing only the difficulties that any change would impose on other aspects of her life and the lives of her husband and children.

7. *Where You Will Find Yourself: Ten of Swords*

The Ten of Swords depicts a prone figure run through by ten swords. It dramatically tells of the end of something, although the card does not mean a physical end. The Ten of Swords in this position suggests that Catherine will find herself increasingly in need of a change, for this card indicates that a change is more or less inevitable due to internal rather than external forces. The butterfly that hovers next to the figure suggests rebirth and heralds a new phase of life.

8. How Others See You: Three of Swords

The heart pierced by three swords, although certainly not a cheerful image, does represent a release of tension. Coming after the Ten of Swords, the Three of Swords represents some sort of a resolution to the problem. While all change is trying at best and painful at worst, it does at least mean that after a period of feeling stuck, things can at last move forward. It seems probable that Catherine's situation will change in some way and that other people will interpret the events that take place in her life more negatively than she will herself.

9. Your Hopes and Fears: Nine of Wands

This card shows an embattled man fighting to protect what he has. It indicates that there will be a struggle but there will be strength and energy in reserve. This suggests that, although life might get tough for a while, any difficulties can be overcome. Catherine felt that she both hoped and feared that changes would occur in her life. She realized that any changes would inevitably present difficulties initially but she thought that she would be able to deal with them.

10. The Outcome: Knight of Pentacles

The Knight of Pentacles is a secure and stable Knight who makes his way across a ploughed field in a measured way. The suit of Pentacles is linked to the earth element, and Catherine was cheered by the image of this Knight as it indicated emotional and financial security. The Knights all signify journeys, and therefore changes, but the Knight of Pentacles is the most careful and considerate of the four. As it appeared in the final position, it seemed to indicate that Catherine could look forward to some stability and security after the immediate turmoil either through her own concentrated efforts or with the help of someone else who has the qualities embodied by this Knight, of perseverance and industry.

THE MAJOR ARCANA

The Major Arcana is composed of twenty-two cards, which together describe all the stages of a person's life. The journey through the procession of the Major Arcana cards is The Fool's journey through life. The Fool, like each of us, must pass through childhood and adolescence until he finally enters adulthood where he encounters the four virtues of Justice, Temperance, Strength and prudence (The Hermit). At this point, he must face mid-life and the crisis that this so often evokes, signified by The Wheel of Fortune. The second half of life involves some inner soul searching, represented by The Hanged Man, Death, The Devil and The Tower. Once he has reached a deeper understanding of himself, he can proceed to a meeting with the higher principles, represented by The Star, The Moon and The Sun. This results in rebirth, in the Judgement card, and finally in triumph in The World.

As you study the imagery of each card, try to 'feel' the image deeply within, to connect with it. If you can attach your own emotions to each card in some personal way, it will help increase the depth of your understanding. As with the Minor Arcana, detailed analysis is provided for each of the cards, drawing attention to the symbolism contained in each image. Possible divinatory meanings are also discussed. At the end of the section a sample seven-card Star spread reading is presented that relates to the Celtic Cross reading at the end of the Minor Arcana section. This reading uses only the Major Arcana and illustrates how to link individual card meanings to create a cohesive 'story'. Finally, a sample five-card reading, using the whole deck, is laid out, showing how to combine both the Minor Arcana and Major Arcana in a single reading.

THE FOOL

The butterfly symbolizes the soul

The white rose stands for passion and purity

The cliff represents the threshold of a new phase

THEME *The urge to change overcomes the fear involved*

The Fool is the card that starts the cycle of the Major Arcana. He is depicted as young, carefree and innocent of the dangers that may befall him if he does not look where he is going. His position at the edge of a precipice is like that of the child waiting in the womb to be born: he is about to walk off the cliff into earthly life. His face is upturned and he is following a butterfly, which, in classical pagan art, symbolized the soul. In one hand he holds a stick with a bundle attached to it, representing his past, which he does not need at present as he is standing on the edge of a new phase life. In the other hand he carries a rose, symbolizing passion, which is white, the colour of purity. He is as yet unaware of the nature of his quest or where his journey will take him. His dog looks up at him questioningly, as if to ask where they are going, but The Fool ignores him. He is too busy experiencing the pleasure of the moment to make plans.

Divinatory Meaning

The Fool embodies a fresh start, and the beginning of anything new usually evokes ambivalent feelings. At the start of a new venture, you may experience feelings of excitement mingled with fear; a sense of looking forward to something that might prove interesting coupled with doubt and anxiety.

When The Fool appears in a reading, it means quite simply that something new is about to occur. It may be that a new opportunity is about to come into your life, or it may be that you can no longer tolerate the status quo and need to break free from the current situation. Take a look at The Fool about to walk off the edge of the cliff: it is a potentially perilous action, yet he is joyous and confident. His dog is trying to warn him of the potential dangers ahead but The Fool takes no notice. While you may not be clear exactly how your life should alter, when The Fool appears in a reading you will be sure that the old way is no longer satisfactory and that a risk must be taken to facilitate a change.

THE MAGICIAN

One hand points up towards the heavens while the other points towards the earth, showing him as a link between the two

The snake eating its own tail is a symbol of eternity

The four symbols of the Minor Arcana reflect the four elements

Lemniscates are the symbol of infinity

THEME *New beginnings, opportunities and talents*

The Magician card shows a dark-haired man, under a flow-ered arch of red and white roses in a garden full of white lilies and red roses. The white lilies represent purity of spirit and the red roses passion and desire. Together they represent unity and balance. The fertility of the garden reflects The

Magician's own infinite potential. He wears a white tunic, indicating the purity of his intentions, and a belt composed of a snake eating its own tail, a symbol of eternity. His crimson cloak suggests that he is aware and accepting of his desires. He stands with his left hand, the side of creativity, holding his Magician's wand, which he points upwards towards the heavens, and his right hand, the side of action, pointing down towards the earth. The Magician acts as a bridge between the two spheres. Before him stands a table, the edge of which is decorated with lemniscates, the mathematical symbol for infinity. On the table stand the four emblems of the Minor Arcana: the Pentacle, the Cup, the Sword and the Wand, which in turn represent the four elements of earth, water, air and fire.

Divinatory Meaning

The Magician is a card of great energy and potential, as suggested by the emblems available on the table. In a reading, it means that new opportunities are available to you. To take advantage of these, a decision has to be made about which path to follow. You may wish to go down the material path (Pentacle), the emotional path (Cup), the intellectual path (Sword) or the creative path (Wand). The Magician offers you the choice and the decision is yours.

Following The Fool, who does not always know what his options are, The Magician is a guide: he points out directions and offers ideas, but he never takes responsibility for the choice. Flashes of knowledge, premonitions or clues about which way to go are provided by The Magician within us, but because he is also a trickster, we are sometimes nervous about following the path his spirit wants us to take.

THE HIGH PRIESTESS

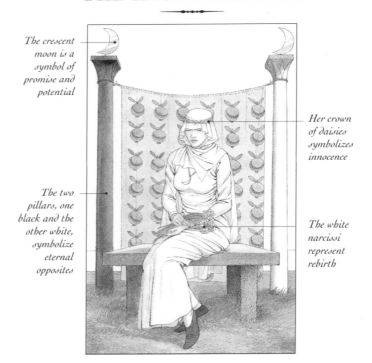

The crescent moon is a symbol of promise and potential

The two pillars, one black and the other white, symbolize eternal opposites

Her crown of daisies symbolizes innocence

The white narcissi represent rebirth

THEME *Secrets revealed, mysteries uncovered*

The High Priestess reveals a beautiful young woman who sits between two pillars, one white, the other black. She is the middle point who holds together the eternal opposites: day and night, masculine and feminine, creation and destruction. At the top of each pillar rests a crescent moon, indicating the early stages of a cycle. The High Priestess wears simple white robes, symbolizing her purity. Her crown is made out of white daisies, the flowers of innocence. A curtain decorated with pomegranates, the many-seeded fruit of love and fertility, hangs between the two pillars. On her lap lie white narcissi, the flowers associated with death and rebirth.

Divinatory Meaning

The High Priestess is a mysterious and fascinating image. She sits before a curtain beyond which a glimpse of water can be seen, yet there is no clear image of what else might be there. The world of The High Priestess is filled with vestiges of ideas that can only appear in consciousness as dreams or intuitions and are difficult to piece together into a coherent pattern. The water signifies the unconscious, which contains many hidden treasures. The High Priestess sits between the pillars of opposites; between the conscious and unconscious. She is like a filter through which creative ideas and intuitions can pass.

The High Priestess can be seen as the feminine side of The Magician. In a reading, this card suggests that it is a time for uncovering secrets and finding out about previously unknown aspects of both yourself and life in general. The High Priestess is linked with the new moon, which in turn is linked with the virgin, a symbol of unrealized potential. So when this card appears in a reading, it can mean that something is gestating in the depths of your unconscious and, although you may be aware that something is happening, it is not possible to know consciously what it is until the moment of its birth. The High Priestess must be approached with patience and sensitivity, otherwise she will not reveal her secrets.

THE EMPRESS

The waterfall cascading into the river suggests the union between male and female to form a child

Her crown has twelve stars for the signs of the zodiac

The corn is a symbol of the fruitfulness and fertility of the earth

Her necklace is made of ten pearls, one for each of the planets

THEME *Creativity, fertility and relationship*

The Empress depicts a beautiful woman seated in a golden cornfield. The corn is a symbol of fruitfulness and fertility, over which The Empress presides. At her feet sits the Horn of Plenty filled with the earth's rich offering of food, and she holds a sheaf of barley on her lap. The Empress is an image of creativity and her robes are full to hint at a pregnancy. She is the Queen of Nature, and her dress is embroidered with the red roses of passion and hemmed with leaves. Her necklace is composed of ten pearls, one for each of the planets that comprise our solar system, and her crown has twelve stars, one for each sign of the zodiac and for each month of the year. Behind her is a waterfall cascading into a river, suggesting the union between male and female to produce a child.

Divinatory Meaning

The Empress represents creativity of a natural, earthy kind. She is the mother who gives birth and nurtures her young, bringing them lovingly to maturity. In a reading, her presence may indicate the possibility of relationship, marriage or family, or it may relate to the creative process involved in writing, painting or any other artistic pursuit. The Empress represents the obvious and material result of the hidden process of gestation symbolized by The High Priestess.

The Empress presides over the daylight world. The bulb of the narcissus is nurtured in the dark world of The High Priestess until it is ready to emerge into the light world of The Empress. The High Priestess is the new moon, virginal and full of promise, while The Empress represents the full moon and potential fulfilled. Together they encompass both the shadowy and the bright face of the feminine. When The Empress appears in a reading, she signifies a time of abundance, fertility and domestic stability. She represents the sense of security and contentment that can be achieved through physical comfort. She suggests the satisfaction that is gained from bringing something to fruition.

THE EMPEROR

His gold crown is a symbol of worldly authority

The Emperor's robes are red and purple, the colours of power and majesty

The barren hills represent the sterility of a world based only on authority and discipline

The eagle on the shield symbolizes the spirit encased in the material world

THEME *Authority, ambition and material stability*

The Emperor is pictured sitting on his square throne of worldly status, which is decorated with eagles. Eagles are royal birds honoured with the power to fly higher than any other bird and with the keenest eyesight. Beside The Emperor is a shield engraved with the emblem of an eagle, symbolizing the human spirit encased in the material world. His throne is angled towards the right – the side of action. He holds an orb in his left hand, the side of creativity, as a symbol of his understanding of the laws of the material world. The sceptre in his right hand serves as a symbol of his masculine potency. His robes are red and purple, the colours of power and majesty, and his heavy gold crown is a symbol of worldly authority. The barren hills behind him symbolize the sterility of a masculine world founded entirely on authority and discipline.

Divinatory Meaning

If The Empress portrays Mother, so The Emperor represents Father. The Empress represents the power of the body and the natural world, while The Emperor symbolizes the power of the mind and the social world. Together they form a balanced whole. The Emperor in the tarot reflects the traditional masculine authoritative position and structured role. He uses his mind and logic to solve problems and address issues.

The Emperor is depicted as a figure of power and influence: he is dressed in the purple robes of majesty and wears the crown of authority. His function is to organize the world for both himself and others. So, when The Emperor appears in a reading, it suggests that it is time for you to take material control over your world. This might be in terms of creating or changing jobs or even buying property. The Emperor indicates the kind of energy that is required to make definite changes or to bring ideas into concrete reality. He represents discipline and direction, and is a helpful influence if you need to make any practical moves at work or at home because his energy is about moving things on and making things happen.

THE HIEROPHANT

The triple-tiered crown symbolizes body, mind and spirit

His raised hand reflects the expression 'as above, so below'

The crossed keys of gold and silver represent the masculine and feminine joined in harmony

THEME *Search for spiritual meaning*

The Hierophant means High Priest and is the masculine counterpart of The High Priestess, representing the spiritual side of the masculine. He sits between two pillars because he too represents a balancing force between the opposites of masculine and feminine, day and night. He wears simple white robes, symbolizing purity of spirit, and a crown made up of three tiers, symbolizing the three states of being – body, mind and spirit – and an understanding of the physical, emotional and mental spheres. Around his neck The Hierophant wears a chain with crossed keys. One key is gold for the masculine spirit and one is silver for the feminine, and together they form a balanced whole. He holds his left hand up with the first and second finger pointing upwards, and the third and fourth fingers folded on to his palm and held in place by his thumb. This is an expression of 'as above, so below', meaning that what is on earth is a reflection of what is in the heavens.

Divinatory Meaning

While the true origin of this card has not been clearly established, its divinatory meaning is certainly one of spiritual knowledge or at least the desire for it and is not limited to a particular creed or doctrine. In essence, The Hierophant represents the urge in man to understand his higher nature.

When The Hierophant appears in a reading, it suggests a wish to find a meaning in life that touches a deeper layer of the psyche than the desire for material success or social status. This could mean that you feel a desire to explore the spiritual side of your nature through study with the aid of books. Alternatively, it may mean that a teacher, mentor, priest or even psychotherapist appears in your life and helps you to explore this spiritual realm. Whichever route you take, the appearance of this card heralds a time when you will not be satisfied with the mundane or worldly aspects of life and will feel strongly inclined to search for an inner meaning and greater purpose in life.

THE LOVERS

Cupid fires arrows of love and hate at mortal's hearts

His yellow shirt reflects mental energy and his blue tunic symbolizes communication

The white dress is the colour of innocence

The deep pink dress is the colour of desire

The rose is the flower of love

THEME *Love and choice*

The Lovers card depicts a young man standing between two women. He looks confused as if at a loss as to which one to choose. He wears a yellow shirt, the colour of mental energy, and a blue tunic, the colour of communication. One of the women is young and fair and dressed in white, the colour of innocence. The other woman is dark haired and a little older, wearing a deep pink dress, the colour of desire. In a cloud above them hovers Cupid, pointing his golden arrow towards the young man. If Cupid fires his golden arrow at a man's heart he will instantly be inflamed with passionate love for the first person he sees. A garden of roses, the flower of love, can be seen in the background. The young man is obliged to make a decision between the two women and to choose one means to sacrifice the potential relationship with the other.

Divinatory Meaning

The card of The Lovers has many facets, all of which need to be considered when interpreting it. Of course, its title, The Lovers, implies that it is connected with affairs of the heart, and indeed it can be, but it is not limited to love alone. The essential meaning of this card is the need to make a choice; to commit to one person, idea, way of life and in doing so refuse another. The obvious interpretation is one that involves choosing between two people, and this is the image used to depict The Lovers in most traditional decks: a young man is confronted with choosing between two women, both clearly different, one older and wiser and the other younger and more beautiful. This card can suggest a choice between mother and lover, or even between 'sacred and profane love'.

When this card appears in a reading, the subject of the choice can be in any area of your life and The Lovers card highlights the need to consider all the ramifications carefully before making a final decision. It is important to remember that sometimes the choice that has, on the surface anyway, great advantages may also have equally great disadvantages.

THE CHARIOT

Mars, the planet of war, is the co-ruler of Scorpio

The black horse pulls in a different direction to that of the white, suggesting tension between the opposites

Red is the colour of desire and aggression

THEME *Struggle and tension*

The image of The Chariot card is of a warrior driving a chariot pulled by two horses, symbols of energy and activity. One horse is black and the other white, representing opposites, such as heart and head, or dark and light. It is the charioteer's task to find a balance between the two. However, as each horse is pulling hard in different directions, the chari-oteer has great difficulty in keeping control of them. He is a symbol of the ego under siege from the rest of the personality's conflicting emotions. The charioteer is dressed for battle and wears a cloak of red, the colour of desire. In the background lies an empty battlefield filled with dust, while overhead the clouds are dark and the sky looks threatening.

Divinatory Meaning

The Chariot is a card that describes the personality in a state of struggle, eventually resulting in triumph. The struggle is essential to reach a higher state but once the higher state is reached, another challenge is likely to appear and so the cycle repeats. It is only through struggle that we can grow and change. The different-coloured horses represent the different problems that co-exist within us that we must all face if we are to keep our conflicting feelings and thoughts in balance. The difficulty the charioteer faces is how to pull all the differing thoughts and emotions together sufficiently to proceed in one direction.

When this card appears in a reading, you might feel that you are having to face the difficulty of feeling one thing yet knowing logically that you ought to do something contrary to that feeling. How do you manage this contradiction and how do you decide which thought or feeling to follow? Can you compromise, as the charioteer is attempting to do by encour-aging both horses to give way a little to join a middle path? The appearance of The Chariot indicates that the time is ripe for the conflicting – and possibly even aggressive – forces within to be recognized and processed so that progress can be made.

JUSTICE

The curtain is purple, the colour of wisdom

The sword of truth is held upright in the hand of action

Her dress is green, the colour of love and healing, while her cloak is red, the colour of passion and purpose

Her headdress is yellow to reflect mental communication

Her scales represent the ideal of perfect balance

THEME *A balanced mind found through logic*

Justice depicts a figure seated between two pillars, representing justice and mercy, before a curtain of purple, the colour of wisdom. She holds a sword, representing truth, upright to reflect the idea that wisdom cuts through illusion to reveal true meaning. She holds the sword in her right hand, the side of action, while in her left, the side of creativity, she holds a pair of scales, which represent the ideal of perfect balance. She wears a red cloak, symbolizing passion and purpose, over a green dress, the colour of healing and love. Together they represent a balance. Beside the figure of Justice perches an owl, the bird of wisdom, known for its clear vision and ability to see in the dark.

Divinatory Meaning

Justice is the first card in the Major Arcana to reflect the four cardinal virtues, the others being prudence (The Hermit), Temperance and Strength. Justice, with her sword of truth and scales of equity, encourages us to pay attention to our thoughts and to understand the need for logical thinking. Justice seeks perfection and equality, symbolized by the sword and the scales, which are also symbols for the masculine and feminine. Justice represents our unique capacity for discrimination and analysis, using the power of the mind.

When Justice appears in a reading, it indicates that the time is ripe for weighing up a situation, using logic and reason, rather than the emotions or intuition, to find an equitable solution to any problems. The card may relate literally to a court case or legal matter, or simply to a decision in your life that needs to be made using impartial rather than emotional judgement. Justice is a virtue, and as virtues are also ideals, it means that its aims can never be completely realized. The true aim of Justice is to achieve fairness and equality, which is an impossible dream in an unfair world. Nevertheless, it is necessary to keep aspiring to it because it is the only way to continue to make improvements in society.

TEMPERANCE

The rainbow
is an image
of promise

The angel pours
the waters of
feeling from
the gold cup,
symbolizing
consciousness,
to the silver
one, which
stands for the
unconscious

The triangle
represents the
body, mind
and spirit

The pool of
water stands for
the inner world
of feelings

THEME *Cooperation and sharing*

Temperance depicts a figure with rainbow wings, pouring
liquid from a gold cup into a silver one. The silver represents the feminine and the unconscious. It is the metal of the
moon and the cup is held in the left hand, the side of creativity. The gold cup represents the masculine and consciousness.

Gold is the metal of the sun and is held in the right hand, the side of action. The flow between the two cups represents the need for flow between the conscious and the unconscious.

On the front of the angel's robes is a golden triangle pointing upwards contained within a square. This symbolizes the spirit's ability to rise from within the physical body. Around the head of the angel is a silver star attached to a golden band, another indication of the balance between the feminine and masculine. The angel stands with one foot on dry land and the other in water, suggesting an ability to link the inner world, symbolized by the water, with the outer world represented by dry land. In the distance stand twin mountain peaks, the path between them representing balance. The rising sun suggests new hope for the future and the rainbow is an image of promise and symbolizes hope.

Divinatory Meaning

Like Justice, this is a card of balance. Justice represents balance through the mind, Temperance the need for balanced emotions. The water poured from one cup to the other represents the need to continually blend feelings. Temperance (one of the four virtues) suggests that moderation is the key to contentment. When Temperance appears in a reading, it indicates success in relationships because of its emphasis on exchange with others in an equitable way. It suggests that it is a good time to concentrate on feelings and relationships. Feelings need to be constantly shared, so they do not stagnate. The water moving from one vessel to another reflects the angel's role as mediator between the conscious and the unconscious self, as well as the emotions between one person and another.

STRENGTH

The sun reflects masculine energy

Red roses and white lilies combine the masculine and feminine harmoniously

The lion is a powerful solar animal, symbolizing masculine strength and aggression

Her white robes symbolize the moon and feminine energy

THEME *Inner courage and strength*

The card of Strength reveals a beautiful woman wearing white robes of innocence. In her hair she wears red roses and white lilies, symbolizing desire and passion combined with spiritual purity. The woman is subduing a lion by holding its jaw open as if to calm the beast and render it harmless. The woman in white reflects the lunar or feminine principle, while the yellow lion represents the solar or masculine principle. There is a constant need to find a balance between the two. The image of a very feminine-looking woman struggling with a very masculine-looking lion is a curious one, yet there is a powerful sense of the inner strength of the woman being matched by the outer strength of the lion.

Divinatory Meaning

When Strength appears in a reading, it may seem obvious that it means that strength is either required or available in a particular situation. While this is true, it is important to remember that the strength reflected by this card is not necessarily physical. Although the card shows a woman in combat with a lion, Strength is not just about winning a fight in a literal sense; it is also connected with an inner struggle. In the image, the woman is not trying to kill the lion; she is seeking to prevent him from being destructive. She holds open his jaw to stop him biting or struggling. She does not want to quash his energy; she only wants to stop him from being injurious.

In terms of personality, the lion is a symbol of the self-interested 'I want' drive, which we all possess and need to ensure survival. However, we also need to keep it in check if we are to successfully co-exist with others.

In a reading, Strength describes the process that takes place when we have to control urges without repressing them. The woman symbolizes inner courage and self-discipline. These are virtues that we would do well to acquire as they provide us with a means of using powerful energy, symbolized by the lion, in a constructive rather than destructive way.

THE HERMIT

Unlike The Fool, The Hermit keeps his eyes down at the path below

The lantern represents the inner light

His staff is used to support him on his difficult journey

The snake is a symbol of transformation

THEME *Patience and prudence*

The Hermit card shows an old man with a long white beard, symbolizing age and wisdom. He walks along a stony path in a barren landscape with a dark sky. The only illumination emanates from his lantern, which represents the inner light. His simple robes are designed for travel and he holds a staff for support on his journey. His face is turned down, as he keeps his eyes firmly on the path. The Hermit can be seen as the Fool at the mid-point of his journey. The Fool starts out blithely, using his staff to carry a bundle over his shoulder, looking up, rather than where he is going. He is the image of carefree, trusting youth. The Hermit is older and wiser. He uses his staff to steady himself and is aware of the potential difficulties that lie ahead. The snake at his feet symbolizes transformation, as it sheds its skin of youth and grows a new one in old age.

Divinatory Meaning

The Hermit is the card of patience and maturity. His lantern suggests that no matter how bleak life may get, he has spiritual illumination to keep him on the right path. The Hermit is linked with the fourth virtue of prudence, suggesting that he has learned caution and vigilance from personal experience.

When The Hermit appears in a reading, it suggests that you might need time to withdraw from the outer world and turn inwards. It is a time for meditation and inner understanding. This card does not signify a lack of relationship, but points to a desire to spend time on your own, examining your inner life. This card symbolizes a shift in perception, like the transition when moving from youth to middle age. The Hermit suggests a deep acceptance and understanding that life does not remain the same and youth does not last forever. Once this concept is absorbed, it brings a sense of peace and tranquillity. The Hermit offers wisdom and patience and a new appreciation of life, which is only truly precious when we realize how fleeting it is.

THE WHEEL of FORTUNE

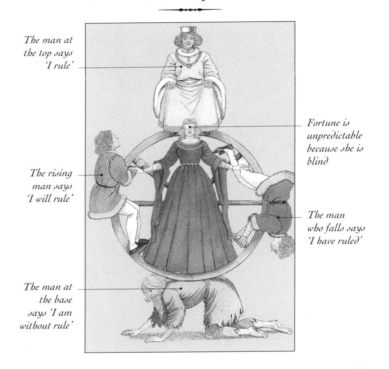

The man at the top says 'I rule'

Fortune is unpredictable because she is blind

The rising man says 'I will rule'

The man who falls says 'I have ruled'

The man at the base says 'I am without rule'

THEME *Changes in fortune*

The Wheel of Fortune shows Fortuna, goddess of chance. She turns the wheel of life, making our fortunes rise and fall, and, although she wears purple, the colour of wisdom, she also wears a blindfold, indicating that fortunes unfold haphazardly. She stands in the wheel with arms outstretched. A man holds on, anticipating reaching the top as it turns. Another man approaches the bottom of the wheel. At the top sits a crowned man, looking proud and safe; while at the base an unfortunate man who has fallen off altogether crawls in shame. Each man is attributed with a motto. The man who rises says, 'I will rule'; the man at the top says, 'I rule'; the man who falls says, 'I have ruled' and the man at the base of the wheel says, 'I am without rule'. This image demonstrates the four phases of life to which we are all subject: times of good fortune and opportunity and times of strife and poverty.

Divinatory Meaning

The Wheel of Fortune reminds us that we have both control and no control over our lives. We have control in that we can choose between various paths and actions to take. We live our lives treading a cautious line between fate and free will. It is possible that what seems random and fated may be part of a pattern, so that an incident that initially seems to be a disaster may turn out to be the proverbial 'blessing in disguise'.

When The Wheel of Fortune appears in a reading, it means that circumstances are changing; it heralds a new phase in life reflecting either an upward or downward turn of the wheel. The wise man is one who accepts the downturns with grace because he knows that the wheel will turn again and that he will rise in the fullness of time. The truly wise man knows that there is never a run of luck that does not run out, whether positive or negative. The Wheel of Fortune does not indicate which way fortune is heading. This can sometimes be gleaned from the surrounding cards and also perhaps from your own feeling about your life at the moment the card appears.

THE HANGED MAN

Twelve branches stand for the twelve signs of the zodiac

His red stocking stands for passion and the white stands for purity

His leg forms an inverted triangle, showing the descent of the higher to the lower

His shirt is green, which stands for love and healing

The pool represents the unconscious mind

THEME *Sacrifice*

The Hanged Man is shown hanging between two trees. Each tree has six cut-off branches, representing the twelve signs of the zodiac. The foot on the right side of his body (the side of action) is bound, revealing that the man is in no a position to act. His red and white stockings represent passion and purity; his green shirt symbolizes love and healing; his red tunic, desire. His arms behind his back symbolize his commitment not to act; while his left leg is bent to form an inverted triangle. This is a symbol of the higher descending into the lower, consciousness into the unconscious. The pool of calm water beneath him represents the unconscious world over which he is suspended. His face is serene and peaceful, his eyes open and unafraid, and a halo-like glow encircles his head, suggesting the light that shines in the darkness.

Divinatory Meaning

The Hanged Man is a curious image and one in which the position of the central figure looks rather uncomfortable. This card is not violent, however: the upside-down position represents looking at life from a different point of view. If you look carefully at the figure you can see how calm and contented he appears. The Hanged Man represents the need for a new outlook on life, and suggests a voluntary sacrifice.

When The Hanged Man appears in a reading, it suggests a need to examine your ideas according to your current experience. In order to do this it may be necessary to let go of some things in order to make way for others. Making a sacrifice means relinquishing something armed only with the hope and belief that something more valuable will take its place. Sacrifice is a voluntary act and one that only you can choose to undertake: no one can force you to make a sacrifice and you must assume responsibility for whatever decision you make. The Hanged Man suggests the need for descent into the unconscious in order to discover what is truly important, so that you may know how you want to change your life.

DEATH

His headdress is made of the death shroud that was once the swaddling cloth of birth

Beauty, youth, majesty and holiness mean nothing to Death, who claims all at the right time

The raven was seen as a harbinger of death

THEME *Transformation and change*

A skeleton riding a black horse (the colour of death) is the image of Death. He carries a scythe, usually used for reaping the harvest, and an hourglass, indicating that everything on this earth has its own time, both for life and death. Around the skeleton's skull is a thin headdress made from a shroud that was once the swaddling cloth of birth. Directly in the path of Death a king lies face down on the ground, while a bishop, a beautiful woman and a child all beg Death for mercy. These figures symbolize that Death comes to all.

A raven, thought to be a harbinger of death, and a few poppies, the flowers of death, are shown. In the distance winds a river, a symbol of the eternal process of transformation: the river water evaporates, turns into clouds, which then return to the river as rain. The little boat is a symbol of the cradle and coffin, life and death, which are inseparable. The sun is rising, indicating the birth of a new day after the death of night.

Divinatory Meaning

Many people fear the Death card for fairly obvious reasons. However, when Death appears in a reading, it means that something must end, but it does not mean a physical death. The endings that Death signifies are many. For example, it might symbolize the end of childhood or the death of single life when you marry; the end of a job or a marriage.

All these endings are linked with new beginnings too, represented by the sun rising over the river, a symbol of the constant process of renewal and transformation. The skeleton is a symbol of the underlying continuation of life: although the flesh may change, the bones remain fundamentally the same. We can see Death in the seasons as every autumn the leaves fall and die to make way for new buds in the spring.

When Death appears in a reading, it suggests that something is dying to make way for a new beginning, which can be both sad and necessary, and both unwanted and welcomed. It is a symbol of change and transformation.

THE DEVIL

The Devil keeps man imprisoned by his own laziness and apathy

The Devil inflames man's base desires

The man and woman have become creatures of the Devil by growing horns and tails

The chains around their necks are loose and their hands are unbound so they are able to free themselves

THEME *Power and energy imprisoned*

The image on The Devil card is of a strange-looking man whose lower body is that of a goat. He has horns and leathery wings. He is seated on a block, symbolizing the material world, attached to which are two chains shackling a naked man and woman. Both have horns and tails, suggesting that they have adopted the Devil's ways. The Devil's torch is touching the man's tail and could set it on fire. Chains loop around the necks of the man and woman, but their hands are free. This indicates that they are voluntarily enchained to the Devil through their own ignorance, apathy or lack of consciousness. The black background suggests that it is difficult to see the truth. The couple are slumped at the Devil's feet and do not appear to want to make any effort to alter their restricted lives.

Divinatory Meaning

The Devil is a card that arouses fear, yet the message it brings is one of release. The Devil has become connected with, among other things, the evils of sexuality, leading to attempts to repress sexual urges. Repression means to push something into the unconscious, which can be dangerous. After all, if something is conscious we have a choice about how to handle it.

The Devil refers to all that is dark in your own psyche. This is why we like to think of The Devil's abode as deep within the bowels of the earth in a place so safely removed from us that we do not have to deal with him. However, such an attitude also means that we live in fear of The Devil, and remain chained to his block of inhibition, restricted because we cannot face the truth about ourselves.

In a reading, The Devil provides us with an opportunity to be free from the bondage of our own fear, and release positive energy. It allows us to examine what is really going on inside, to look under the surface more closely. The Devil's appearance means that blocks and inhibitions in the psyche that restrict healthy expansion can be removed, allowing great progress to be made on an inner level.

THE TOWER

The flames indicate the divine fire of inspiration which dispels false values

The falling man and woman represent unreconciled opposites

The narrow windows reflect the narrowness of a purely material life

THEMES *Demolishing the old to make way for the new*

The Tower card shows a tall building in a raging sea. Waves lick the bottom of the Tower and storm clouds gather in the dark sky, while vivid flashes of lightning strike the top. The flames seen raging from the roof represent the divine fire needed to demolish false or inappropriate values.

The Tower is the only card that uses a man-made object for its central theme; the external constriction of internal development. It is a tall imprisoning building that restricts expansion and growth. The lightning that shatters it is divine enlightenment striking so that the self may not be suffocated. Large drops fall from the heavens, which represent the life-saving food of inspiration and enlightenment. Three narrow windows stand near the top of the Tower, indicating the narrowness of the material and rational world, as well as the possibility of high attainment. Two figures fall from the Tower, representing unreconciled opposites and separateness: the fall of human beings kept apart by lack of communication and understanding.

Divinatory Meaning

The Tower is an image of necessary destruction. It suggests a constant need for the redefinition of values, and that courage will be needed to change them if they are no longer appropriate. The divine lightning, representing knowledge and enlightenment, may come in the form of change or disruption from outside, or from within when you find you cannot bear to continue with your present way of life. The more in tune you are with your inner world, the less traumatic the effect of The Tower is likely to be. In fact, it can represent a welcome release, shattering illusions and highlighting values that no longer mean anything to you.

The Tower encourages us to face our inner worlds honestly, sifting through what we have been taught and the rules by which we have lived to discover if they are still valid. The Tower provides the inspiration that helps us sort out what elements must change, to clear away the old and make a fresh start.

THE STAR

Eight stars represent the number eight of rebirth

The ibis is the bird of immortality

The evergreen tree represents everlasting life

The figure is naked to represent truth unveiled

The water falls in five streams to represent the five senses

The pool is the Pool of Memory

THEME *Hope and inspiration*

The Star card depicts a beautiful woman kneeling beside a pool of water. She is naked to represent truth unveiled and young to represent renewal. She has one foot in the water, representing the future, and the other on dry land, representing the past. She also acts as a link between the conscious and the unconscious. The pool represents the Pool of Memory from which we need to drink to remember life-sustaining events.

The Star maiden pours water freely from two pitchers, one into the pool to replenish it and the other on to the ground to revitalize the land. The water separates into five streams, symbolizing the senses. In the distance stands an evergreen tree, representing everlasting life, with an ibis, the bird of immortality. The ibis is a symbol of the soul's ability to rise above everyday levels of emotional and spiritual understanding. In the dawn sky, symbolizing the birth of a new day, a huge Star appears surrounded by seven smaller stars, which symbolize the seven ancient planets. All the stars have eight points as eight is the number of rebirth and resurrection. There are a few white roses and daisies growing nearby, indicating purity and innocence. A butterfly, symbol of resurrection, passes by behind her.

Divinatory Meaning

The Star has long been seen as a symbol of hope: the light used by sailors to navigate their course, and by astrologers seeking heavenly guidance. In a reading this card represents the radiance that glows in the dark, giving us courage to maintain a positive attitude even when times are hard. If we lose hope we become despondent and feel inclined to give up the struggle. It also represents optimism and encouragement, and the dreams and goals we strive for. In a reading, The Star suggests rejuvenation, inspiration and the renewal of energy, which make life worth living and goals worth aiming for. Without such inspiration and hope life becomes meaningless and empty.

THE MOON

The moon's three faces show the three phases of woman

The dog and the wolf howling at the moon represent the animal side of the personality

White lilies and roses, lunar flowers, grow by the pool

Cancer is the astrological sign ruled by the moon, and its symbol is the crab

The pool is the Pool of Forgetfulness

THEME *Fluctuation and confusion*

The Moon card shows three phases of a large Moon, which hangs in the centre at the top of the image. Each phase corresponds to one of the three faces of the feminine. The new Moon represents the virgin whose potential is unfulfilled; the full Moon represents the mother whose potential is fulfilled;

and the old Moon represents the old woman whose potential is used up. The dog and the wolf represent the unconscious 'animal' part of the personality, released under the lunar influence. Two pillars on either side of the pool represent the conscious and the unconscious mind, and the path in between that leads from the water towards the meeting place of mountain peaks in the distance is the path of balance. The deep, still water represents the Pool of Forgetfulness, lying to the left of the Pool of Memory depicted in The Star card. This pool is also a symbol of the unconscious but represents the experiences we prefer to forget. Cancer is the astrological sign ruled by the Moon and its symbol is the crab. A crab is crawling from the water, bringing information from the dream world to consciousness. White lilies and roses, lunar flowers, grow near to the pool.

Divinatory Meaning

The Moon rules the night and therefore The Moon in the tarot is a card of darkness and uncertainty. The Moon rules darkness and dreams, the waxing and waning rhythms of life, and is linked to all natural cycles.

In a reading, The Moon suggests a period of uncertainty and fluctuation. It rules volatile feelings, so unstable moods may be expected. Situations seem more serious in the dead of night. Dreams are not easy to decipher, and yet if you take the trouble they can be very rewarding indeed. When The Moon appears in a reading, nothing can be taken for granted, nor should firm decisions be hurried. Because The Moon suggests confusion, it is tempting to make a quick decision in order to end the uncertainty. However, it may be wise to let events take their natural course rather than forcing the situation.

THE SUN

The sky is clear blue, symbolizing clarity of vision

The straight and wavy rays of the sun symbolize both its positive and negative effects

The child is an image of new life

Sunflowers and heliotropes are solar flowers

Oranges are solar fruit

The laurel hedge represents the need for boundaries

THEME *Joy, optimism and clarity of vision*

The Sun card shows a child wrapped in a brilliant red scarf, symbolizing passion, riding a white horse. This is the horse that was ridden by the skeleton of Death, but this time it is white to represent life. The child, an image of renewal, rides the horse triumphantly through a garden of sunflowers, small orange trees heavy with fruit and heliotropes: all solar plants. The Sun shines brightly, its rays straight and wavy, suggesting they can have both positive and negative effects: the Sun can ripen fruit and turn pasture into desert. A laurel hedge, representing success, surrounds the garden, indicating the need for boundaries. The blue sky symbolizes that the situation can be deciphered now the darkness of night has been dispelled. The joyful child represents freedom from the restriction of the night.

Divinatory Meaning

The Sun rules the day, brings clarity of vision and a sense of optimism and positive energy. Imagine worrying in the dead of night and remember the anxious feelings that surface when the Moon rules. Now, imagine the dawn breaking, and the Sun rising in the sky, feel the warmth of its rays and the fear draining away. Suddenly what seemed impossible at the darkest hour seems possible again. This is the gift of the Sun.

In life there must be limits, which is why the Sun and Moon need each other. Too much solar energy can be exhausting, and the Moon is needed for rest and recuperation. By the same token, too much lunar darkness leads to depression. We need the Sun and Moon in equal proportions to achieve a healthy balance.

In a reading, The Sun brings a strong sense of enthusiasm and exhilaration: the Sun's energy is of the 'can do' variety. Nothing seems impossible when The Sun comes up, and even if it appears alongside more difficult cards, its joyful energy has a positive influence that permeates the reading. It suggests an emphasis on action and positive thought, and indicates a time of strength, good health and general good cheer.

JUDGEMENT

The trumpet calls the dead to rise

The white flag with a red cross symbolizes the meeting of opposites at the centre point of reconciliation

The child is an image of the mystery of the new self we are about to become

The sea is a symbol of the waters of the womb

THEME *Resurrection and resolution*

The Judgement card shows three naked figures rising up from their tombs – a man, woman and a child – with arms outstretched and faces lifted towards an angel. They are naked because that is how we come into the world. The child has its back to us, and symbolizes the mystery of the new self we are about to become. The tombs are surrounded by the sea, symbolizing the moment between life and death and between death and rebirth. The water reflects the waters of the womb in which new life is protected until birth. The joyful rise of the figures symbolizes the moment of birth, of triumphant release from darkness. In the clouds appears a winged angel wearing white, the colour of spiritual purity. The angel blows a trumpet to call the dead to rise, or the unborn to be born. Attached to the golden trumpet is a white flag with a red cross on it. White is the colour of life and red is the colour of purpose. The middle point of the cross symbolizes the meeting of opposites, which are reconciled at that point where everything that has been separate join as one.

Divinatory Meaning

Judgement is the penultimate card of the Major Arcana. It is a summation of what has been experienced and achieved through the previous cards. Judgement is known as the card of karma, because it heralds the time of reaping what has been sown. There are moments in everyone's lives when the outcome of a situation can be seen in direct response to how it has been handled all along. Sometimes we are pleased with how things turn out and at other times not so pleased. In a reading, this card indicates that the moment has arrived to make an assessment, to judge your own actions and appraise how you have done. It does not refer to the final judgement, but rather to a culminating point in life when choices have to be made in readiness for the next phase, with the departing phase kept in mind. The Judgement card suggests that something of such a karmic nature requires attention.

THE WORLD

The winged man stands for the zodiac sign of Aquarius

The eagle stands for the zodiac sign of Scorpio

The gold crown symbolizes attainment

The laurel leaf symbolizes success

The winged bull stands for the zodiac sign of Taurus

The winged lion stands for the zodiac sign of Leo

THEME *Achievement, success and completion*

The World card shows an oval wreath made of laurel, the leaf of success, tied with the red ribbon of achievement. An odd figure dances in the middle. Naked but for a purple scarf, (the colour of wisdom) draped to conceal the genitals, it is a hermaphrodite. The World card represents completion and harmony, so the figure combines both sexes to symbolize unity. In each corner is an emblem of each element – earth, fire, water and air – and a representation of the four fixed signs of the zodiac: Taurus the Bull, Leo the Lion, Scorpio the Eagle and Aquarius the Man. A combination of all four elements would result in a perfect fifth, which is symbolized by the central dancing figure who holds a wand in each hand – one black, the other white – reinforcing the theme of duality, which is constantly repeated throughout the tarot. The gold crown on the figure's head represents attainment. The oval shape of the wreath echoes the figure zero, symbol of all beginnings and endings. It is also reminiscent of the womb from which all life emerges. At the end of the procession of trumps, all is complete. At this point the dancing figure becomes the foetus in the womb waiting to be reborn again as The Fool.

Divinatory Meaning

The World is the final card of the Major Arcana and represents completion. At the point when the World is realized, the journey must start again. So goes the story of every man's life. We do not reach a certain point of achievement and then stop. Following completion is the need to proceed to the beginning of the next thing. The new always evokes The Fool and the journey will inevitably evoke the essence of the other cards.

In a reading, this card means that a moment of completion or attainment has arrived. This may take many forms: the passing of exams, the occasion of a marriage or the birth of a child, to name a few. Whatever the moment of achievement referred to, it is certain that after the triumph there must be a regrouping in order to start again on a new journey.

Sample Reading for Major Arcana

T*he Star spread reading uses cards of the Major Arcana only and forms the second part of my structured reading programme, continuing Catherine's exploration of her situation, begun with the Minor Arcana reading (see pages 136–40).*

Catherine wanted to explore her own needs and desires at a deeper level, to understand how she could make life more fulfilling without harming her family relationships. Should she turn away from career and focus more on her family? This presented the problem of how a reduced income would affect their situation. She was also unsure that such a life would be intellectually stimulating or grant her enough status.

Catherine selected seven cards from the Major Arcana only, and I laid them out in the Star spread as follows:

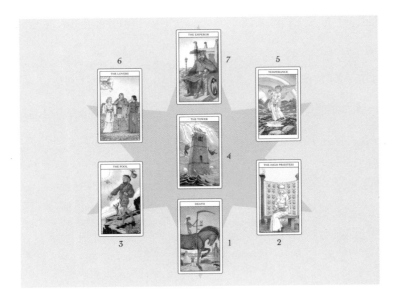

1. Root of the Matter: Death

The Root of the Matter is the emotional starting point for the reading. The card shows Death passing through the landscape unmoved by the entreaties of those along the way. It highlights the fact that change happens whether we want it to or not. This echoes the Ten of Swords in the first reading (*see page 159*), and suggests change within Catherine.

Catherine was becoming aware of the fact that her children were growing up. The end of one stage makes way for a new one to begin, and she felt that the next stage as a mother may be less demanding. At the same time she felt sadness that those precious baby days were over. Death marks a time of transition, and Catherine was able to feel both optimistic and nostalgic as the change took place.

2. Emotions and Relationships: The High Priestess

This is a subtle card that suggests potential unfulfilled. Catherine was conscious of the need for change in her relationships, yet did not want to push through changes aggressively. The High Priestess seemed to connect with the Seven of Swords in the Minor Arcana reading, which indicated a need to wait for the right moment. The High Priestess encourages the use of intuition to guide you rather than intellect. It also indicates that the secrets hidden in your unconscious will be revealed only when you are ready to understand them.

3. Intellect and Career: The Fool

The Fool pushes for change and adventure. The fact that this card appears in the place of Intellect and Career reveals that Catherine feels a greater desire to alter her work pattern than she does her relationship with her family, represented by The High Priestess. The two cards work in very different ways: The Fool seizing new opportunities and The High Priestess advocating contemplation. A balance between the two must be struck.

4. Heart of the Matter: The Tower

The position of this card in the reading stresses its importance. It highlights the need to dismantle old structures. If you ignore its energy, it can erupt violently, but if you work with it, it can be very cleansing and refreshing. The Tower urged Catherine to scrutinize her ideas and beliefs and be prepared to abandon the old to make way for the new.

5. Unconscious Influence: Temperance

Temperance is a peaceful card with the gentle angel an image of sharing, compromise and cooperation. It would take compromise between Catherine and her husband to agree on a new lifestyle. Temperance is an excellent card to have in a reading as it symbolizes compromise and honest communication. It indicates that a satisfactory agreement would be achievable.

6. Conscious Influences and Desires: The Lovers

The Lovers card represents the need to make a choice. Catherine did not feel that her choice was about people, but was questioning her family's direction. This card enhances the Seven of Cups in the first reading, which indicates a range of choices, whereas The Lovers limits the choice to two options and suggests that decisions will be made using emotion, not logic.

7. Top of the Matter: The Emperor

This card represents the outcome for the present and is one of stability and ambition. The Emperor is a powerful image, depicting someone who rules his kingdom confidently. It showed Catherine that she must find a practical solution to her dilemma. The Fool's energy must be balanced with careful thought. The Emperor indicated that a new career would afford greater material reward and status, or that a person characteristic of The Emperor would play a part in it.

Sample Reading for Complete Deck

The final part of Catherine's three-part reading uses the whole deck in the five-card Horseshoe spread. This spread provides an overall summary of the previous two readings — it is the culmination of the entire reading. I find that this method of first looking in detail at the everyday nature of a person's life, then looking closely at the psychological or spiritual aspects, and finally using all the cards in a summation of the situation, provides a very full picture of what is happening at a particular point in a person's life.

Having explored all the issues, gaining more insight into what was going on in her own personal inner development, and understanding more precisely the nature of the choice presented to her, Catherine was eager for a summation of the reading. She wondered if any of the cards seen in the previous two readings would reappear. Often, cards important to the seeker make a reappearance in the final reading.

Catherine selected five cards from the whole deck, and I laid them out in the Horseshoe spread as follows:

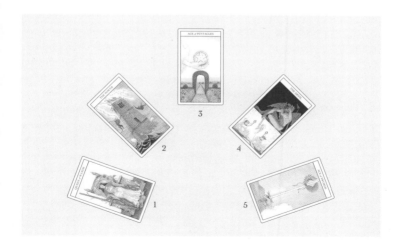

1. Present Position: Queen of Wands

The Queen of Wands represents a person who is capable of successfully doing a number of different tasks at the same time. This certainly described Catherine, who was at once keeping hold of the domestic reins and running a business. She often felt she was juggling the different elements of her life, keeping several balls in the air at once. The Queen of Wands is able to manage this by being creative and industrious, and by focussing her abundant energy precisely. She is also a realist, knowing her limits and tolerating a degree of imperfection rather than expecting the very best all the time. The Queen of Wands is linked with the fire element and she therefore has enough enthusiasm and optimism to carry her through difficult times. The appearance of this card showed that Catherine was managing her life well at the moment, despite her feelings of frustration.

2. Present Expectations: The Tower

It is interesting that the central card from the previous reading, The Tower, also appears in this final reading. It emphasizes The Tower's importance in Catherine's life at the moment. As we saw in the first reading, Catherine was aware of feeling trapped by her current lifestyle. She was sure that this could only be changed by restructuring her life and therefore that of her family. In many ways her main obstacle was her husband's fear of tackling the situation. Catherine herself was fearful of upsetting him and of rocking the boat generally, but her feelings of restriction were becoming more and more acute, and she realized that they would soon reach a degree that she could not accept emotionally. When this moment arrived, she knew she would have no choice but to instigate change, whatever the consequences. She did expect The Tower, which part of her feared and part of her welcomed, as she knew it would bring with it a release of tension and a more honest relationship with herself and her husband.

3. *What is Unexpected: Ace of Pentacles*

The Ace of Pentacles reveals a new beginning materially, so it seemed that something might occur financially that would give Catherine more options when deciding the best route to take. She was encouraged by the thought of a proposition that might alter her material fortunes, especially as it might give her the opportunity to make a fundamental shift in her life without compromising the financial security of the family. This card may also indicate an unexpected job offer or the funding to develop her business.

4. *Immediate Future: The Devil*

The Devil is a card that demands attention. In this position, The Devil seemed to be requiring Catherine to think seriously about herself and her own needs and motives in order to understand where her desire for change was coming from. The Devil is a card that forces you to be honest with yourself and ignoring it can put up barriers that make life uncomfortable. When The Devil appears in a reading, his dark world should be confronted, after which life will be a lot smoother. We tend to avoid dealing with awkward issues, but when we are forced to confront them and have the courage to deal with them, we usually feel better, releasing a lot of energy that would otherwise be repressed.

5. *Long-term Future: Ace of Swords*

The Ace of Swords marks a new beginning, bringing with it a sense of sweeping change. This may seem disruptive initially, but it is necessary for life to move on. Catherine was pleased with the two Aces in the reading because she felt they heralded changes both in financial matters and in her lifestyle. The Ace of Swords is a powerful card that points to a positive outcome once the challenges that accompany change have been courageously met. It might be that Catherine's new beginning does not look very promising at first, but ultimately the new path she takes will prove entirely satisfactory.

Acknowledgements

Many thanks to Ian, Nick, Elaine, Liz, Jane and Barbara for all their hard work and inspiration, and to Giovanni for creating such a beautiful deck.

Juliet Sharman-Burke is a practising analytic psychotherapist. She has been using the tarot and astrology for over twenty years, and has taught both subjects since 1983. She has written several books on the tarot, including *The Complete Book of Tarot*, *The Mythic Tarot Workbook*, *Understanding the Tarot*, and *Mastering the Tarot*. She is also co-author with Liz Greene of the bestselling classic deck *The Mythic Tarot* and *The Mythic Journey*.

Giovanni Caselli is a full-time illustrator with a passion for the classical world, its literature, art, symbols and myths. He has a deep knowledge of history and archaeology that enables him to create illustrations of the past accurate to the last detail. His characteristic line-and-wash style is the perfect medium for the tarot, where colour and detail have symbolic significance.

EDDISON • SADD EDITIONS

Editorial Director Ian Jackson
Commissioning Editor Liz Wheeler
Copy Editor Jane Laing
Editor Nicola Hodgson
Proofreader Michele Turney
Art Director Elaine Partington
Mac Designer Brazzle Atkins
Production Karyn Claridge and Charles James